Jack Tworkov

Red, White and Blue

March 6 – April 13, 2002

Mitchell-Innes & Nash

1018 Madison Avenue   New York 10021   212/744 7400

Ameringer/Howard/Yohe

20 West 57 Street   New York 10019   212/445-0051

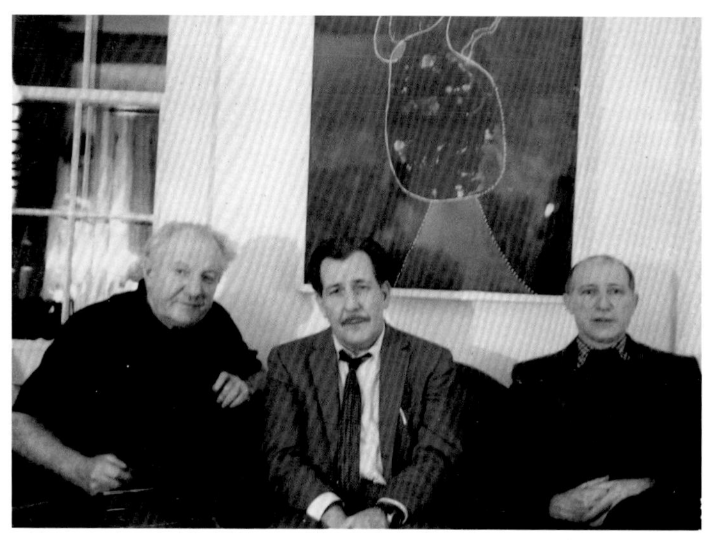

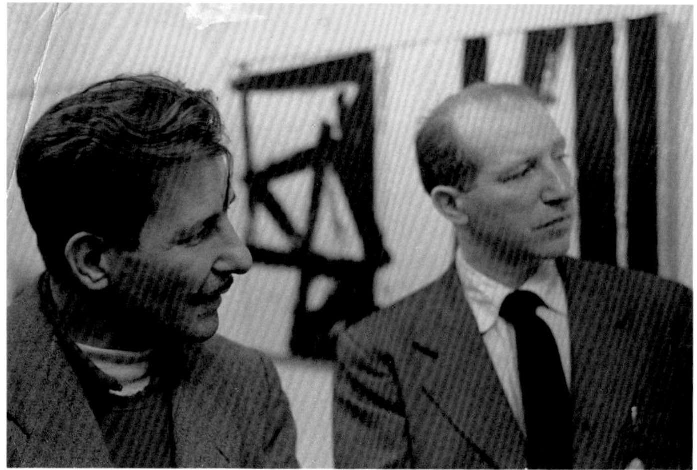

TOP: Hans Hofmann, Franz Kline and Jack Tworkov in Provincetown, circa 1958

ABOVE: Franz Kline and Jack Tworkov, circa 1958

A Compound Eye: Thoughts on Tworkov's Flags

Harry Cooper

FIRST THINGS FIRST. It will be hard to experience this exhibition without recalling September 11th, if only because of the U.S. flag. The flag has been more present in our visual diet since that day than probably at any other time in our history. No doubt it is simply chance that several of Tworkov's flag-inspired paintings are being shown now, within six months and several miles of the attack. But rather than dismiss this coincidence and suppress whatever ahistorical reactions it might elicit, we can turn it to our advantage, for these paintings emerged from another time when the flag was very much in evidence, the late 1950s, the years of "I like Ike" and the post-war boom, the rise of television and the triumph of suburbia, the bus boycotts and the Voting Rights Act—another time when the flag was waved like a talisman at whatever might disturb the American Dream.[1]

The image of the flag floated easily into the visual language of the mid-century avant-garde, but not always as a sign of national pride. Jasper Johns's first flag painting (1954–55) was a lightning rod. Against a backdrop of bravura patriotism and bravura brushwork, its deadpan cobbling of encaustic, newspaper strips, and cotton sheets became, intended or not, the driest of critiques. (After seeing *Flag* in Johns's debut show of 1958, Alfred Barr wanted to acquire it for the Museum of Modern Art, but, fearing the trustees would find it unpatriotic, arranged for Philip Johnson to buy it and give it to MoMA years later, in 1973.[2]) There is a

similar mordancy in the way Richard Diebenkorn suspended a flag from the outstretched arm of the figure in his painting *July* (1957), thus relegating the flag to the status of a formal building block, a handy resource for a painter interested in stripes. The flag as underarm.

But it fell to Robert Frank in his photoessay *The Americans* (1958) to take the full measure of the flag. In his hands it became mercurial, by turns opaque and transparent, waving and gathered, noble and sinister. When the American edition of the book came out in 1959 (significantly, a year after the French), it was considered unpatriotic by many, not just because of its imbrication of poverty and seamy politics with family life and leisure but because Frank spread the flag over all of it as a kind of embracing sanction: each of the four sections of the book opens with a flag photo. Framed by Jack Kerouac's introduction and, on the back cover, a collage by Alfred Leslie in which the red stripes of the flag are rotated and made black, perhaps suggesting bars seen against the light, Frank's photos acquire a bracing, Beat sensibility (it's Grove Press after all), critical but not unpatriotic. They take the flag in vain, but all in the name of a larger, truer sense of what the flag should mean.

Leslie, it should be noted, had been using the flag as a motif throughout the decade, sometimes quite explicitly, in paintings like *A Survivor* (1951) and *Flag Day* (1956) and in a number of collages related to the one for *The Americans*. *Pull My Daisy*, the film he and Robert Frank made in 1959

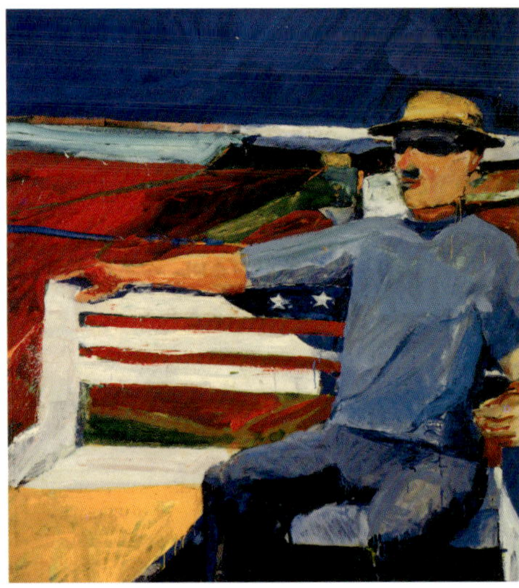

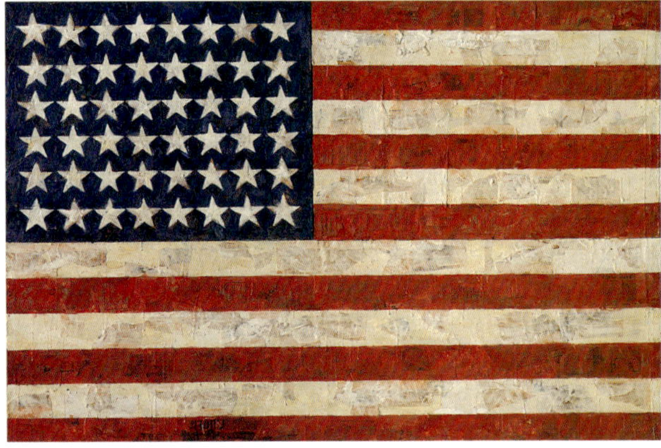

TOP: Richard Diebenkorn, *July*, 1958, oil on canvas, 59 x 54 in. Private collection

ABOVE: Jasper Johns, *Flag*, 1954–55, encaustic, oil and collage on fabric mounted on plywood, 42¼ x 60⅝ in. The Museum of Modern Art, New York. Gift of Philip Johnson in honor of Alfred H. Barr, Jr. Photograph © 2002 The Museum of Modern Art, New York/Licensed by VAGA, New York, NY

with the participation of many major Beat figures, featured a large flag that had been in Leslie's studio for years.[3]

It is impossible to say which of these flags (by Johns, Diebenkorn, Frank, Leslie, or many others[4]) were in the back of Tworkov's mind when he was at work on his five (by my count) flag paintings of 1961–62—the first three *RWB*s (there is a fourth, but it is not really flag-like), *Souza*, and *Oh Columbia*. But we *do* know which one was in front of his eyes: Tworkov had purchased a small Johns flag painting sometime in the late 1950s.[5]

If this fact is surprising now, it was then too. Reviewing Tworkov's 1964 Whitney retrospective for *Art News*, Louis Finkelstein felt the need to explain, speculating that Tworkov "has one of Jasper Johns's flags in his living room to remind him of this particular irony"—the irony that Tworkov in spite of his commitment to painting sometimes "comes perilously close to making just an object."[6] Finkelstein's interpretation seems plausible as far as it goes. As Leo Steinberg wrote in 1961 of the series of painted flags that led up to Johns's 1960 bronze flag-plaque, "The flag stiffens, is slowly hand-painted, and—as the end stage of a process that began with the arrest of its flutter—cast in bronze. The Stars and Stripes forever."[7] Or what Johns himself called "a rigid image."[8] Tworkov, by contrast, seems interested in exactly the flutter. If, like Johns, he tends to fill the field with the flag, it is not to create an ambiguity of art and object, of simulacrum and symbol, but rather to show how the depicted flap of the flag can keep those equations at bay.

But if Tworkov had Johns's flag in his living room as a cautionary tale, it was also a token of mutual friendship and admiration. Johns recalled in a 1977 interview: "The few painters whom I admired and knew when I came to New

York were Philip Guston and Jack Tworkov. I met them during the mid-'50s. . . . I saw more of Jack [than Philip] and visited both his home and his studio. He said some very important statements about painting and I believe that he is one of the least self-centered artists. He is able to look at the work of other people without always thinking about his own."[9] The young critic Michael Fried seems to have known, or more likely sensed, these connections. In 1964, responding to Clement Greenberg's claim in the 1962 article "After Abstract Expressionism" that Johns was mining de Kooning's manner, Fried wrote: "in Johns' early paintings (the first targets, flags, and numbers) the most relevant influences in point of *touch* . . . appear to be perhaps Tworkov and almost certainly Philip Guston rather than de Kooning."[10]

Fried's observation, however critical—it was the "resolute smallness and fussiness" of Johns's brushwork that put him in mind of Tworkov and Guston—is a good corrective to the overwhelming tendency, triggered by the flags, to see Tworkov in the wake of Johns rather than vice versa: "*Oh Columbia* (1962), in red, white and blue, *immediately* recalls Jasper Johns's flags," wrote Sidney Tillim in 1964, no doubt speaking for many visitors to the Whitney retrospective.[11] Tworkov's willingness to appear to follow in the footsteps of such an instantly famous example, even to let it be known that he had an exemplar in his living room, reflects his unusual attitude to influence: "No artist is an artist by himself. He is an artist only by virtue of the fact that he voluntarily permits other artists to act on him, and that he has the capacity to react in turn . . . . Instead of being in a constant state of anxiety, he can be in a constant state of absorption."[12] Not that this attitude puts Tworkov above all petty feelings,[13] but it does seem to explain his ability to maintain simultaneous associations with a wide range of artists in the late 1950s, from Franz

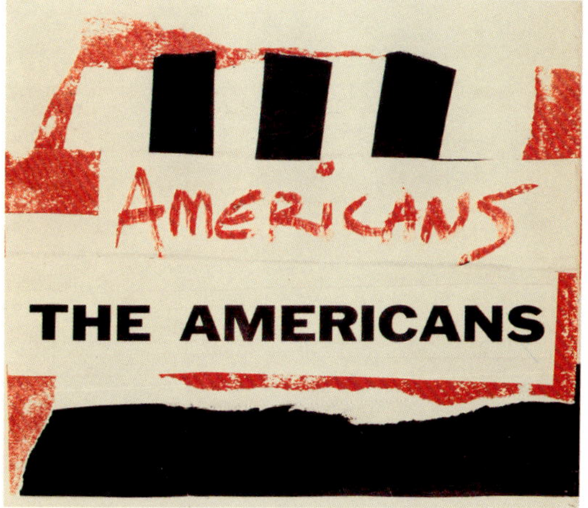

Alfred Leslie, *Flag*, 1959, collage © Alfred Leslie, courtesy the artist

Kline and other Ab Ex peers to Jasper Johns and Robert Rauschenberg to the figurative artists associated with the nascent New York Studio School.[14]

Rauschenberg was another artist with whom Tworkov had a bout of action and reaction; in fact, it must have been through Rauschenberg that he got to know Johns. Rauschenberg studied with Tworkov and Kline ("two of his heroes"[15]) at Black Mountain College in the summer of 1952, and Tworkov, who was 25 years older, took the young artist under his wing. While Rauschenberg was traveling in Europe and Africa in 1952–53, Tworkov stored several of his delicate black paintings for him, then brought him to the attention of two important dealers, Eleanor Ward of the Stable Gallery (where Rauschenberg showed with Cy Twombly in the fall of 1953) and Charles Egan of the Egan Gallery (which he joined in 1954).[16] All this coincides exactly and suggestively with Tworkov's liberation from the influence of de Kooning in these years.[17] It is as if Rauschenberg's famous act of erasing a de Kooning drawing in 1953 were the outward expression of an inner struggle that Tworkov himself was also going through.

The close Tworkov-Rauschenberg relationship is commemorated by Rauschenberg's inclusion of a Tworkov sketch of a man's face in a frankly autobiographical combine sculpture (*Untitled*, 1955, Los Angeles Museum of Contemporary Art)[18]—and also, perhaps, by a reciprocal gesture: the 1960 Tworkov drawing with collaged American flag included here (plate 1). Rauschenberg's hand is not present in this piece, but it might as well be. The inclusion of newsprint, the note of Americana, the dashy violence of the mark-making, and above all the way that violence is controlled by a strongly implied grid—all these recall Rauschenberg's combine paintings of the 1950s like *Rebus* (1955) or *Canyon* (1959).

This drawing is the light-hearted inauguration of Tworkov's interest in the American flag. The collaged scrap includes a waving flag with (look closer) a jaunty yet authoritative finger extending from a suited arm to point at it. Tworkov seems to underscore the redundancy of this creepy, instruction-manual act of digital exhortation (everyone knows that the flag is there to be looked at, sung at, pledged to, saluted) by echoing the finger with a painted arrow pointing up at the flag from the lower right quadrant of the image. Or perhaps, given the cruciform at the heart of the collage and the general violence of the mark-making around it, the finger belongs to a doubting Thomas, and the flag has or is a wound.

But these readings seem either too cynical or too flippant for Tworkov. A self-described "ghetto-Jew born in Poland" who fled with his family to New York in 1913 at the age of 13, he espoused the unapologetic patriotism of the immigrant.[19] For Tworkov, America was truly a land of freedom and opportunity. He noted in his journal on August 30, 1959 that in the U.S. it was possible "for intellectuals to be patriots" and concluded the entry with "America is the hope of the world." If the artistic vanguard of the 1950s was generally imbued with the spirit of Arthur Schlesinger's 1949 book *The Vital Center*, as Serge Guilbaut and more recently Michael Leja have argued, no one embodied it better than Tworkov.[20] When he writes (on 3/15/59), "I am for the extreme of the middle, the creative middle," he is talking about both politics and art. He was as staunchly anti-Communist as he was anti-Fascist. He condemned beatniks and Dadaists but went regularly to the Five Spot, where John Coltrane and Thelonious Monk were making modern jazz history. In short he was, in art and politics, a card-carrying liberal.[21]

But I suspect that Tworkov's inclusion of the collaged flag in this drawing was no more an act of patriotism than of mock-patriotism, but rather just a note to himself: "Look at the flag," the finger enjoins, pointing at it, perhaps even pressing it, thus mimicking the act by which Tworkov himself had affixed the scrap to the page. "It's interesting."

IF I HAVE TARRIED too long at the crossroads of personal and artistic relations where Tworkov meets Johns and Rauschenberg, a crossroads where the flag seems to have been planted, it is because those relations in all their reciprocity are too often forgotten. This has allowed Tworkov to be repeatedly cast as a failed or "fussy" abstract expressionist (by Fried, Tillim, and Donald Judd, to mention some early examples[22]) rather than an artist in search of a different set of coordinates—even if he had to pass through abstract expressionism to get there.

What were those coordinates? Or, to put the question more concretely, What did Tworkov find so interesting about the flag? If the culture at large helped draw him to the flag, a host of formal problems kept him there and continued to interest him through 1965 in several series of related works—problems of texture and space, of gesture and structure, of movement and grid, and ultimately, of drawing and painting.

Let's begin with Tworkov's most literal flag painting, *Oh Columbia* of 1962 (plate 7), in which the red and white stripes and even the blue and white canton at upper left are unmistakably indicated. To make the painting, Tworkov dragged rather thick, unfluid paint across an extremely coarse piece of canvas, giving the picture a muscular tension,

a sense of strong gesture slowed or constrained. This particular facture-feeling, to coin a phrase, is the keynote of the composition too. The top and bottom blue stripes adhere to the edges of the canvas, creating a powerful internal frame whose action the other stripes only gradually and partially escape as they swell toward the center.[23] The result is nearly a sense that the canvas is pinned along the top and bottom and bulging in the middle—nearly, because of course we know the canvas is stretched flat. And so we interpret the swelling as the furling of the flag in the wind, and with that wind the Johnsian prospect of a flag-object (raised both by the running of stripes along the edges and the filling of the field with the image) is, as Finkelstein suggested, swept aside.

And yet the wind-blown movement of horizontal stripes is constrained in turn by three clumps of verticals, each composed of a red, white, and blue stripe. This act of constraint is pure Tworkov: "I see action as engendering an arresting action." (2/2/59) The red and white verticals are among the last strokes applied to the painting, freshly and easily covering the drying layers beneath; but the blue verticals were applied earlier, as we can tell by looking at their fainter lower extremities, which weave under the white horizontals and over the red ones. These lower extensions are like telltale threads in the fabric of the composition, revealing how Tworkov made his flag, or at least its lower half: red horizontal, then blue vertical, then white horizontal, creating another, more subtle kind of space in the composition, not the illusioned unfurling of gesture but the material weaving of pigment.

RWB #2 of 1961 (plate 3), by contrast, has little of this latter kind of space. Here too the canvas is coarsely woven, but this time it does not seem to have inspired Tworkov to emulate it in his facture. Rather, there is a clear sense of discrete layers—what Tworkov defined as *recession* (created by the placement of planes) in opposition to *space* (created by color and light).[24] A red calligraph or two, similar to the spiky, often dual forms of the *Barrier Series* and related works,[25] is caught between a rear barrier of thick blue and white horizontal stripes and a foreground screen of thinner white verticals. The fact that the white occupies two layers, foreground and background, creates some spatial ambiguity, especially in the case of the white horizontals, but this difficulty is quickly neutralized once we realize that the dual location of the white serves, in classic Greenberg-Cubist fashion, to put a lid on the space, to keep it shallow. The substitution of a red stripe for the expected blue one at the bottom of the image is a similarly easy ambiguity. The illusion of a barred cage is so strong (see where the red figure is allowed to poke its finger out just a bit, at the top between the second and third verticals from the right?) that the space threatens to become a cliché: importunate gesture imprisoned by structure.

But an important moment of difficulty, an aporia in our reading, is presented by the anomalous blue lasso. It is "a truly irrational, a rare and unanticipated occurrence" to borrow words from Tworkov. (1/9/59) His vigorous scratching and scrawling with the wrong end of the brush in this area suggests a struggle. Forms have clearly been painted out, and the blue circle has been added at the end, a last-minute inspiration, even after the white bars, which only *appear* to lie on top. (For another example of this trick of blue-white layering, see the lower left panel of *Variables II*, 1964–65, plate 28). It should be noted that this barred circle seems to be an obsession with Tworkov, appearing in several drawings here[26] as well as twice in *Oh Columbia* (where it is beautifully threaded with red and white) and once in its

close relative, *Souza* (1961). In both of these the barred circle stands in for, or translates, the canton of white stars on blue. It's a weirdly personal eruption in the midst of all the structure: I like to think of it as the subdivided eye of an insect, a compound eye.

These flag paintings are not easy. Eleanor Munro, writing in 1963, called them "transitional essays."[27] Richard Armstrong wrote twenty-five years later: "If not altogether successful, the pictures are noteworthy for the search for new forms and a new palette that they imply."[28] There is something ascetic and unremitting about them, which has much to do with the choice of colors. The limitation to red, white, and blue is not a common one in twentieth-century art. Fernand Léger, Jean Dubuffet, and Stuart Davis exploited the combination but always added the counterweight of black or another primary. Almost everyone, it seems, was afraid of red, white, and blue. Part of the problem is the strong association with both the French[29] and American flags, an association cemented for all time by Picasso's 1912 oval painting *"Notre Avenir est dans l'Air,"* where the tricolor bursts onto the ochre and umber Cubist scene to announce the return of color, reinvented as purely local. Ellsworth Kelly is one of the few to have instantiated the triad alone, in the collage *Red, White and Blue* of 1952, which (he has assured me) had nothing to do with flags.

Another problem is simply that the two primaries want the relief of a secondary and white wants the balance of black, but Tworkov refuses. He endowed such refusals with ethical import: "The sensual abandon to a riot of color always means abandoning the hope of being able to think about and control the form of the picture. The contrary means to choose a strict limit of color within which to work." (3/21/60) Tworkov saw the particular combination of blue and white as a means of transcending color to arrive at pure light. He wanted "to paint a picture of light space and movement, but especially of light. But not the orange, red, and purple light of the interior, but the light of the bright sky. The piercing white and blue, to paint white not as ground, but as central to the picture as bursting light." (3/26/62)

The pursuit of light by an entirely different means seems to be the subject of the three black cut- and torn-paper collages presented here (plates 31, 32, and 33). In these rather private experiments, Tworkov happily borrows devices from Newman, Motherwell, and Leslie. The point is not to be original but to see how light can be brought into the black forms. Tworkov accomplishes this by allowing cracks of light to interrupt the black forms and by selectively altering the surface quality of the black paper, both by leaving shiny glue traces (the result of adjustments to the positions of scraps while the glue was still wet) and by tearing the paper against the grain to expose its uncoated, matte fiber along the rips.

Tworkov uses other media to similar ends in the highly accomplished *Barrier Series* drawings, which include studies for the paintings *East Barrier* (1960, Albright-Knox Art Gallery) and *Site* (1966, plate 19). Here (plates 9, 10, and 18) vigorous, imperfect gum-erasing allows the white of the page to eat into the forms, while the modulation of the dark areas is effected by the strange interaction of compressed charcoal and a softer graphic medium. Where the compressed charcoal lies directly on the page, it picks up the tooth of the paper, creating a granular effect, but where it crosses an area of graphite or possibly vine charcoal, it shines in the light. With such snares, Tworkov evolves a

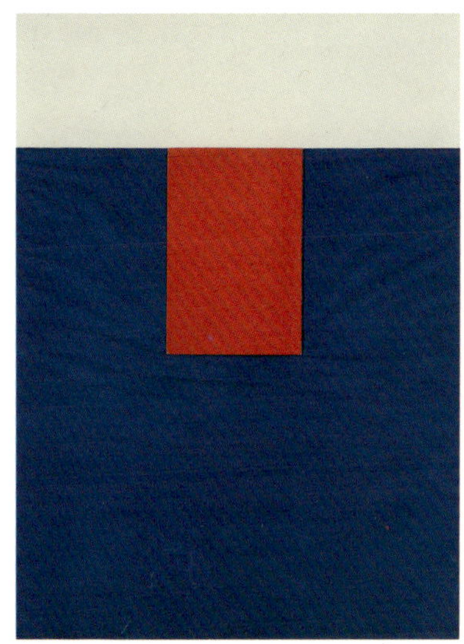

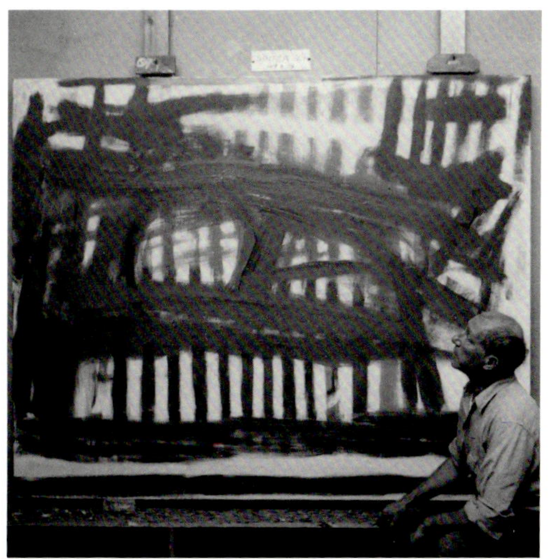

TOP: Ellsworth Kelly, *Red, White and Blue*, 1952, collage, 27¾ x 19⅝ in. © Ellsworth Kelly. Photo by David Matthews, Harvard University Art Museums

ABOVE: Jack Tworkov with *Souza*, circa 1961

whole family of colors from black and white: "For the painter a black and white painting is as much a color painting as a red and green painting." (3/21/60)

These graphic experiments with weaving, texture, and reflectance reached their painted fruition in two major paintings that are almost pendants of one another: *Nightfall* of 1961 (plate 14) and *Barrier Series #5* of 1963 (plate 15). Here a complex color-space is built from a dense weave of individual strokes, drawn with the brush, through which passes a thicker, more manifestly painted element, a stripe or track (white in *Nightfall*, blue in *Barrier Series #5*). But rather than parse these works individually, let me allow Tworkov, always articulate, to speak for them:

> The less the surface is activated by color the more likely it is to be activated by texture. (1/2/54)

> Maybe I'd best define energy as an accretion of consciousness—as distinct from activity which is a mechanical-physical discharge. (1/4/55)

> In a thicket the actors might be lovers, or a murderer and his victim—the anxiety is that of silence of an action without sound, without meaning. (1/2/59)

> Seeing my slides at Princeton made me realize how much of my work is based on linear energy becoming mass. (12/11/59)

Texture, thicket, mass, accretion—it would be hard to find better words (though I would add barrier, snare, weave) for what might be called the drawn density of Tworkov's work, a mode which, as the dates of these quotations indicate, had long been established by the early 1960s.

But with the flags (to return to our theme) comes a shift of interest. "At the end of the fifties, I began to look around for more disciplined and contemplative forms," Tworkov recalled in 1973[30]—began "to break away from 'stroke' painting," as he noted in his journal. (1/28/59) What happens? The thicket clears, the light burns through, an order is imposed, or found—an order of far-sighted clarity, of a flag and its stripes. It does not happen at once: *Oh Columbia* and *RWB #2* seem to weigh, respectively, the claims of the dense thicket with its secret violence and the discrete stripe with its clear structure, with *Souza* and *RWB #3* lying somewhere in between.

This weighing is continued in two unusual paintings, *Variables* of 1963 (plate 27) and *Variables II* of 1964–65 (plate 28). Here the contest of thicket and stripe, and parallel to that, of drawing and painting, is presented in almost didactic fashion, or in the manner of a printmaker's test plate, in which different effects are tried in clearly demarcated areas. The contest is clearest in *Variables*, where the cubicles devoted to drawing actually contain charcoal lines scratched into wet white paint (underscoring the printmaking analogy). In *Variables II*, on the other hand, it appears that paint has been used to give the effect of charcoal, perhaps indicating that the contest has already been decided. The angled midline that spans each painting (ruled in one, painted freehand in the other) emphasizes this dualistic, agonistic content by suggesting a bar dividing numerator from denominator. The reference to fractions is also wholly appropriate to the marks in the right two-thirds of these paintings, which can be thought of as tallies. (Perhaps the spanning diagonal is a kind of fifth tally, the one that binds four together.) Here, for the first time, Tworkov is clearly engaged with simple mathematics, as if he had realized, just after the fact, that the U.S. flag is all about counting. (Stars and stripes = states and original colonies.) The impulse of geometrical division that overtakes Tworkov's work after 1968 is well in the making.

But it would be wrong to say, as I just implied, that the *Variables* decide for painting over drawing. Rather they test the collapse of that opposition, for who can tell whether the thick tally marks are painted or drawn?[31] Tworkov had already thought in deconstructive terms about the opposition, writing that "even a line is merely an extreme aspect of a color shape—and the unpainted surface is another." (1/3/60) Drawing, after all, was not about to disappear from Tworkov's work. The oft-remarked persistence of a not-quite-vertical direction in so many of his paintings from 1950 on (a *tilt* which is almost always thrown into relief by the presence of plumb line: see for example the double white midline in *OC #51* of 1959, plate 13) is nothing other than the characteristic hatching of a right-handed draftsman. What happens to drawing in Tworkov's work around 1965 is not that it is defeated but rather that it is absorbed or sublated. To put it another way, the wind that seemed to blow left to right across so many of Tworkov's paintings (something that *Oh Columbia* wittily thematizes) gets transformed into another kind of movement, less gestural, more structural or musical.

Take *June 21* of 1964, a work in 6/8 time. The painting is divided into six sections or measures, each defined by a group of six red stripes or beats. The exact midpoint of the six-measure phrase, coming between measures three and four, is marked by a white stripe flanked by two lines that are slightly shorter and more orangy than the red stripes. That is the most obvious division of the phrase, and the one that Tworkov soft-pedals. He makes much more emphatic

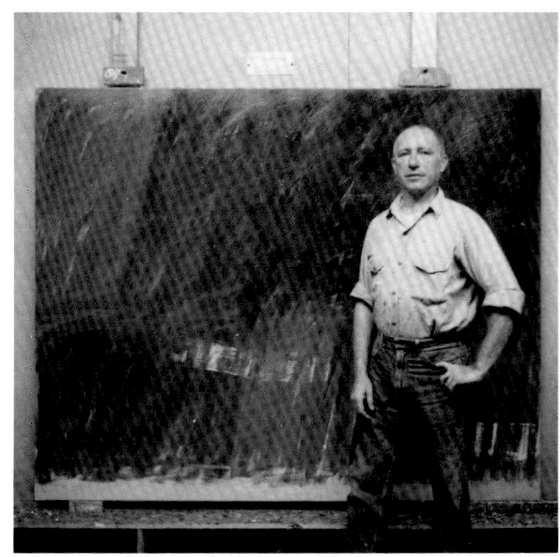

Jack Tworkov with *Nightfall*, circa 1961

divisions after the second and fifth measures (the full-length red bars) and after the first and fourth measures (the shorter white bars). Each of these pairs of bars encloses a three-measure subphrase, one offset to the left of the midline, the other to the right. Other subphrases are marked out by different shades of blue painted between and around the red stripes. All this makes it hard to notice, or even believe, that the white stripe marks the center of the image. It is equally hard to define the space of the image: it is certainly not flat, and yet relations of in-front and behind cannot be defined, seem to have been replaced by relations of prominence—perhaps the equivalent of musical dynamics.

As Tworkov put it in 1973, looking back on the year 1965: "What I wanted was a simple structure dependent on drawing as a base on which brushing, spontaneous and pulsating, gave a beat to the painting somewhat analogous to the beat in music. I wanted, and I hope I arrived at, a painting style in which planning does not exclude intuitive and sometimes random play."[32] Random play: for instance, one of the measures has only five beats.[33]

We have come a long way from the flag paintings of two and three years earlier, or have we? The red-white-blue palette is there to remind us of the connections. So are the titles *Oh Columbia* and *Souza*, both of them musico-patriotic in their reference. Let's give the last words to the song, composed by David T. Shaw in 1843 (and don't forget to obey the repeat in the refrain):

> O, Columbia! the gem of the ocean,
> The home of the brave and the free,
> The shrine of each patriot's devotion,
> A world offers homage to thee.

Thy mandates make heroes assemble
When Liberty's form stands in view;
Thy banners make tyranny tremble
|: When borne by the Red, White and Blue, :|
When borne by the Red, White and Blue,
Thy banners make tyranny tremble
When borne by the red, white and blue.

My thanks to Adrian Turner for his intelligent assistance and to Sarah Boxer for her invaluable editing.

1   For a useful timeline correlating events in politics and culture, see *Forces of the Fifties* (Wexner Center for the Arts, The Ohio State University, 1996), pp. 57–67.

2   Lilian Tone, "Chronology," in *Jasper Johns: A Retrospective* (New York, The Museum of Modern Art, 1996), p. 128, citing Lynn Zelevansky, "Dorothy Miller's 'Americans,' 1942–1963" in *Studies in Modern Art* 4 (New York, The Museum of Modern Art, 1994), p. 104 n. 157.

3   Leslie in conversation with the author, February 12, 2002. For a still from the film, see *Forces of the Fifties*, p. 67.

4   See for example the reproductions in Lucy R. Lippard, *Pop Art* (New York: Thames & Hudson, 1985), p. 20.

5   Richard Armstrong, "Jack Tworkov's Faith in Painting," in *Jack Tworkov: Paintings 1928–1982* (Philadelphia, Pennsylvania Academy of Arts, 1987), p. 26. For a photograph of Tworkov and his wife with the painting in 1975, see p. 141 of that catalogue.

6   Louis Finkelstein, "Tworkov: Radical Pro," *Art News* 63 (April 1964), p. 52

7   Leo Steinberg, "Jasper Johns: The First Seven Years of His Art" [orig. 1962], in his *Other Criteria: Confrontations with Twentieth-Century Art* (London: Oxford University Press, 1972), p. 29.

8   Jasper Johns in a 1965 interview with David Sylvester, in Sylvester, *Interviews with American Artists* (New Haven and London: Yale University Press, 2001), p. 145.

9   Jasper Johns in an interview with Roberta J. M. Olson, "Jasper Johns: Getting Rid of Ideas," *The Soho Weekly News* (11/3/77), reproduced in *Jasper Johns: Writings, Sketchbook Notes, Interviews* (New York, The Museum of Modern Art, 1996), p. 169. See also p. 107 (Johns to Walter Hopps, 1965): "I have admired his

[Tworkov's] painting. I saw a good deal of his work and it was meaningful to me to see it."

10   Michael Fried, "New York Letter," *Art International* (February 1964), p. 60; cited in Fred Orton, *Figuring Jasper Johns* (Cambridge: Harvard University Press, 1994), p. 121. It should be noted that Johns also mentioned several times his admiration for de Kooning.

11   Sidney Tillim, "Voyagers in 'Reality,'" *Arts Magazine* 38 (May–June 1964), p. 27, emphasis added.

12   Jack Tworkov, "A Cahier Leaf: Journal," *It Is* 1 (Spring 1958), p. 25; quoted in Irving Sandler, *The New York School: The Painters and Sculptors of the Fifties* (New York: Harper & Row, 1978), p. 49.

13   "At first you suffer a pang of hurt when you see a painter, especially a friend, take over something you've been working on, all the more so if he gets the credit for it," Tworkov noted in his journal. (2/9/59)

14   In an interview with Paul Cummings, Philip Pearlstein reported that "Jack Tworkov came regularly for almost two years" to a figure drawing group run by Mercedes Matter that included Pearlstein, Charles Cajori, Louis Finkelstein, and others. Paul Cummings, *Artists in Their Own Words* (New York: St. Martin's Press, 1979), p. 163.

15   Mary Lynn Kotz, *Rauschenberg: Art and Life* (New York: Abrams, 1990), p. 76.

16   See Kotz, *Rauschenberg*, pp. 79 and 83; Calvin Tomkins, *Robert Rauschenberg and the Art World of Our Time* (Garden City: Doubleday, 1980), pp. 73, 85, 91, and 107–08; Walter Hopps, *Robert Rauschenberg: The Early 1950s* (Houston, The Menil Collection, 1991), p. 68; and Bruce Altshuler, *The Avant-Garde in Exhibition: New Art in the 20th Century* (New York: Abrams, 1994), p. 167.

17   On this subject see my Tworkov review in *Artforum* 38 (April 2000), p. 139. Armstrong ("Tworkov's Faith," p. 24) notes that Tworkov's "close friendship with De Kooning continued until 1953."

18   Kotz, *Rauschenberg*, p. 87.

19   From a September 24, 1960, letter to Thomas Hess, reproduced in *Jack Tworkov: Paintings 1928–1982*, p. 134.

20   See Michael Leja, *Reframing Abstract Expressionism: Subjectivity and Painting in the 1940s* (New Haven and London: Yale University Press, 1993), pp. 245–49; and Serge Guilbaut, *How New York Stole the Idea of Modern Art: Abstract Expressionism, Freedom, and the Cold War*, trans. Arthur Goldhammer (Chicago and London: University of Chicago Press, 1983), pp. 189–92.

21   I am grateful to Jeri Coppola of the Jack Tworkov estate and Adrian Turner of Mitchell-Innes & Nash for sharing with me selections from Tworkov's unpublished journals of this period. On Tworkov's jazz interests, see Armstrong, "Tworkov's Faith," pp. 25–26. Most serious jazz fans, it should be noted, had little use for the Beats' romanticizing enthusiasm for jazz.

22   In addition to the reviews already cited, see Donald Judd, "In the Galleries," *Arts* 37 (April 1963), p. 55; and Sidney Tillim, "In the Galleries," *Arts* 35 (April 1961), p. 53. For a more sympathetic and perceptive approach to Tworkov, see Dore Ashton's "Art," *Arts & Architecture* 78 (May 1961), p. 5; and "Art USA Today," *The Studio* 163 (March 1962), pp. 84–94.

23   There is even a faint vertical stripe indicated along the far right edge, as if Tworkov were considering extending the internal frame to all four sides, in clear violation of the motif.

24   "It is the intersection of planes (or strokes where they sometimes act like planes) that gives the effect of recession. The effect of recession is not the same as the effect of space." (3/21/60)

25   See especially the *Untitled* gouache (1962), plate 4.

26   One example that may not be readily apparent is the 1965 *Untitled* drawing (plate 24), which conceals two large circles and a number of lines in its dense weave of charcoal.

27   Eleanor Munro, "Tworkov: The Central Image," *Art News* 62 (March 1963), p. 64.

28   Amrstrong, "Tworkov's Faith," p. 26.

29   Fairfield Porter referred to Tworkov's "French-flag blue and red" in his review of the 1961 Castelli Gallery exhibition. See Porter, *Art in Its Own Terms: Selected Criticism 1935-1975* (Cambridge, Mass.: Zoland, 1993), p. 144.

30   Tworkov, "Notes on My Painting," *Art in America* 61 (September–October 1973), p. 69.

31   As if to make that question even harder, Tworkov created the marks in *Variables II* by a complex, counter-intuitive procedure. Not simply light strokes on a blue ground, they are in fact the areas of a light gray underlayer *not* covered by the surrounding blue-gray over blue paint—areas then strengthened in several cases by a final application of white. Once again (as already noted of the lower left cubicle) Tworkov alerts us to the fact that the material space and illusioned space need not coincide.

32   Tworkov, "Notes on My Painting," p. 69.

33   For another counting "mistake," see the drawing *LP #23* (plate 35).

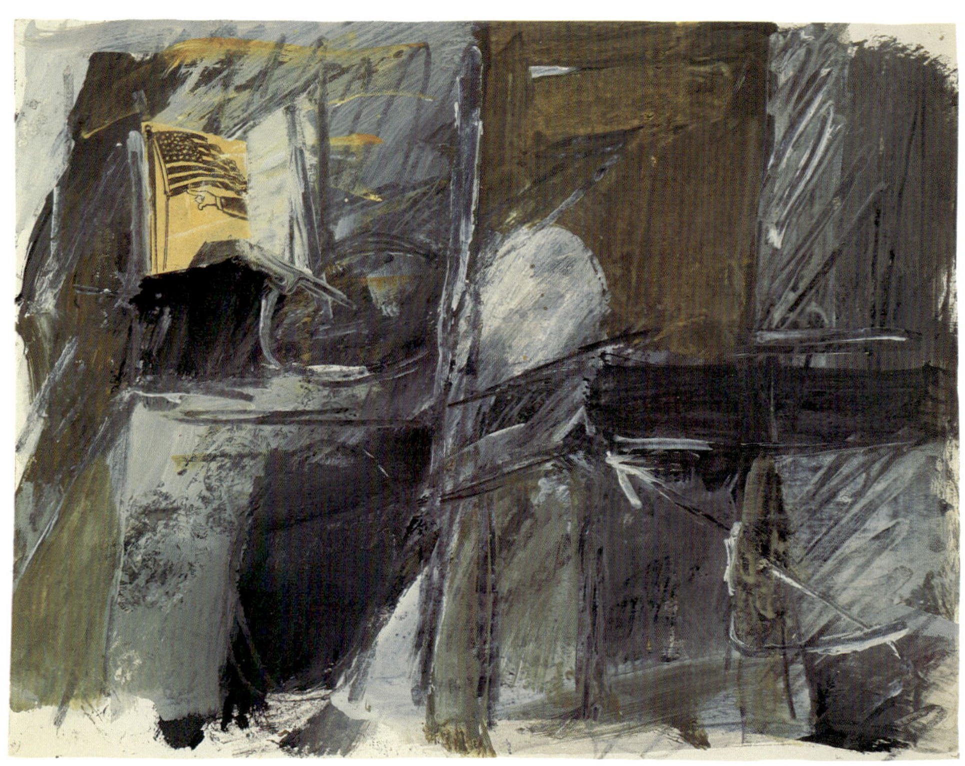

1. *Untitled,* circa 1960. Gouache, pencil and collage on paper, 10⅛ by 12¾ in. (25.6 by 32.5 cm.) †

† EXHIBITED AT AMERINGER/HOWARD/YOHE

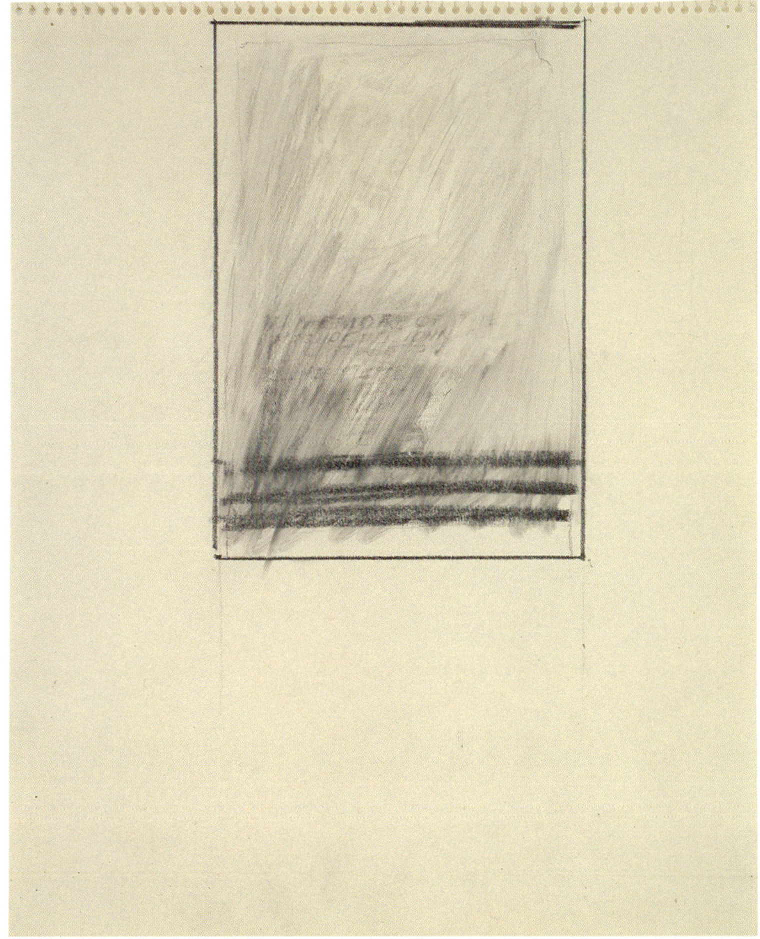

2. *Untitled (In Memory of the President John F. Kennedy)*, circa 1965. Pencil on paper, 13¾ by 10¾ in. (35 by 27.5 cm.) †

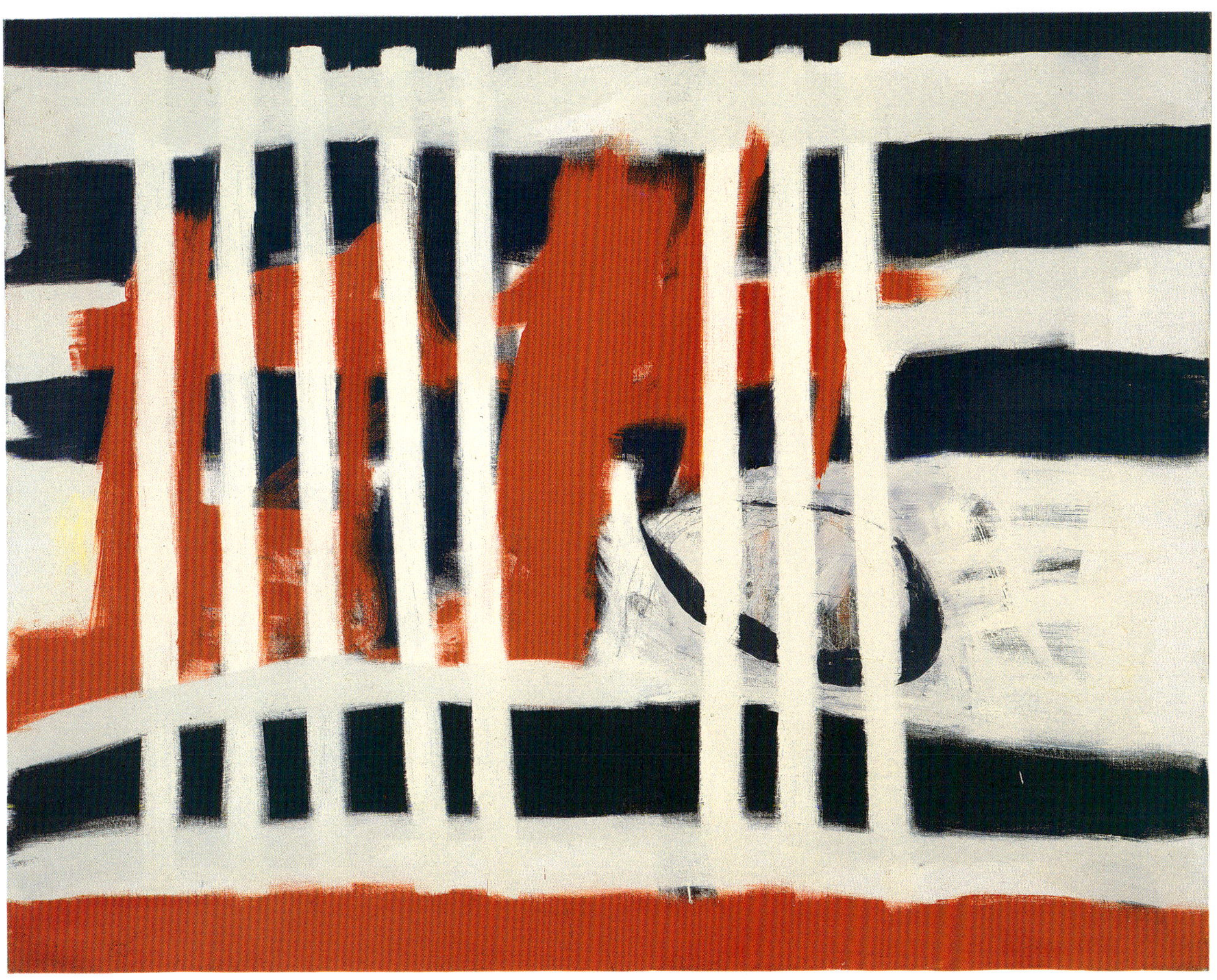

3. *RWB #2,* signed, titled and dated *61* on the reverse. Oil on canvas, 62 by 77 in. (157.5 by 195.6 cm.)

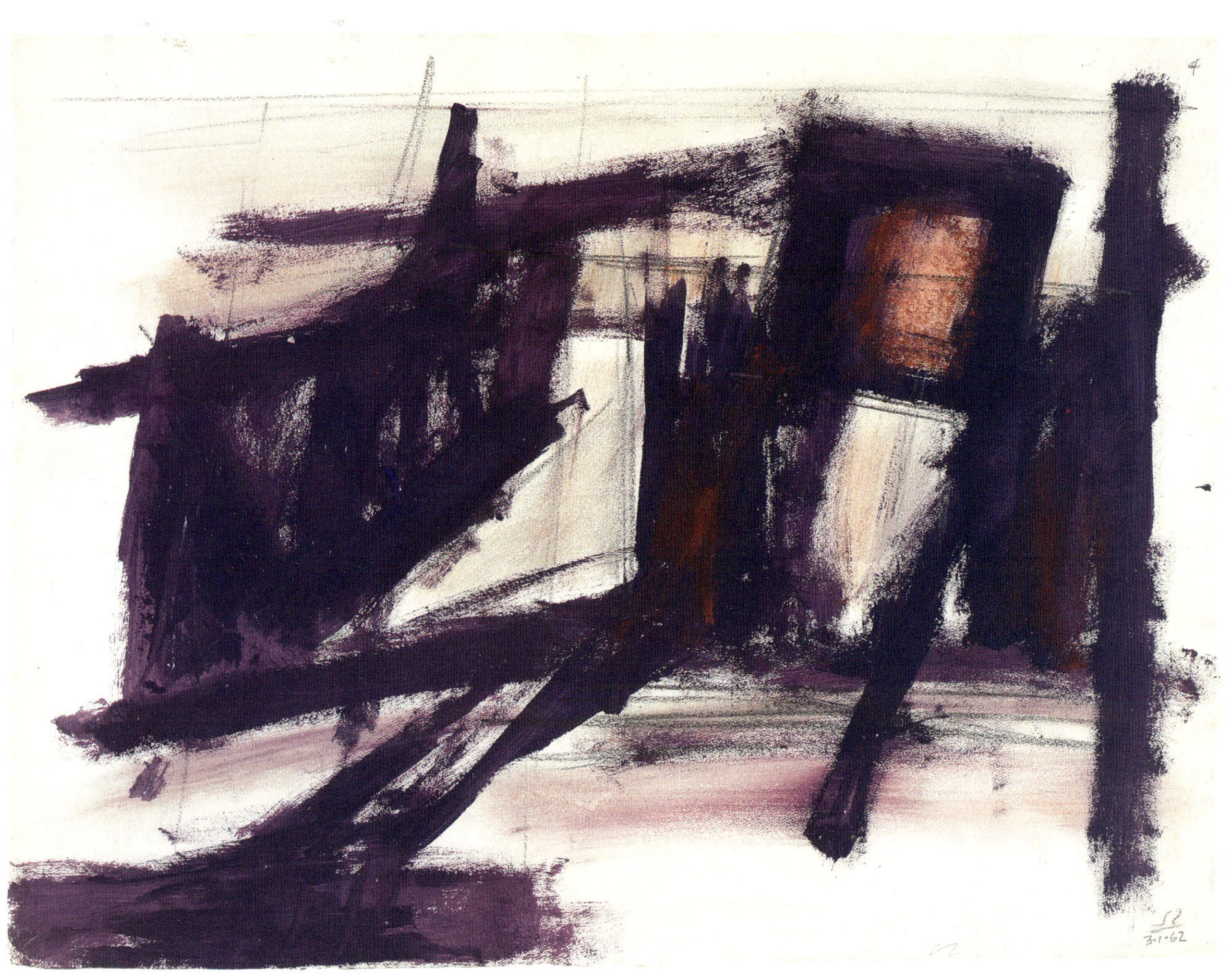

4. *Untitled*, signed with initials and dated *3-1-62*. Gouache and pencil on paper, 20 by 25 ¹³⁄₁₆ in. (50.8 by 65.5 cm.) †

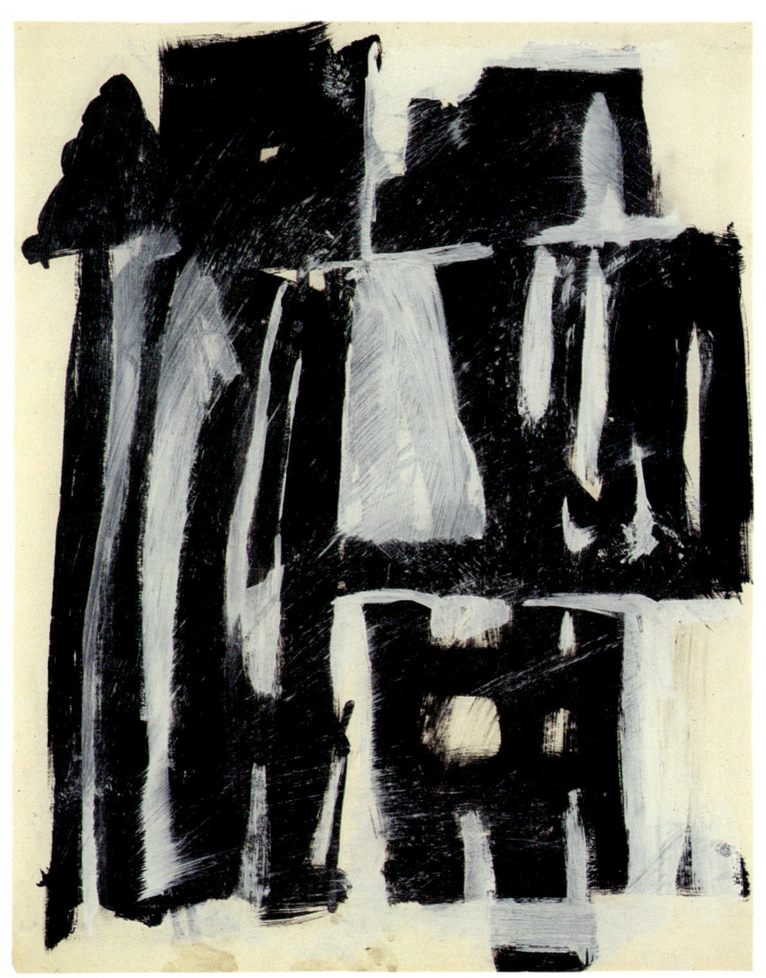

5. *Untitled*, circa 1955–60. Tusche and gouache on paper, 26⅟₁₆ by 20 in. (66.2 by 50.8 cm.) †

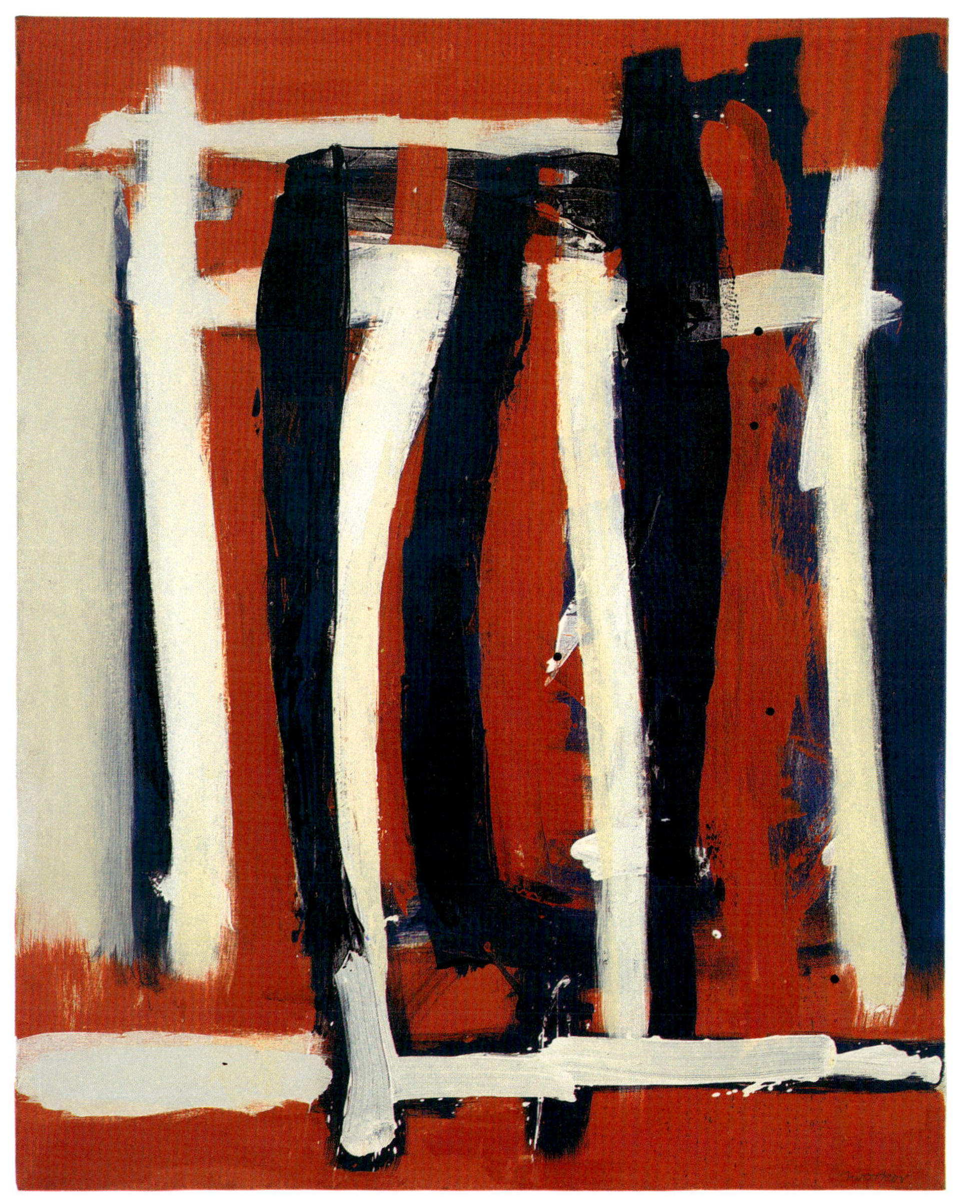

6. *Shield,* signed, titled and dated *61* on the reverse. Oil on canvas, 51 by 40 in. (129.5 by 101.6 cm.) †

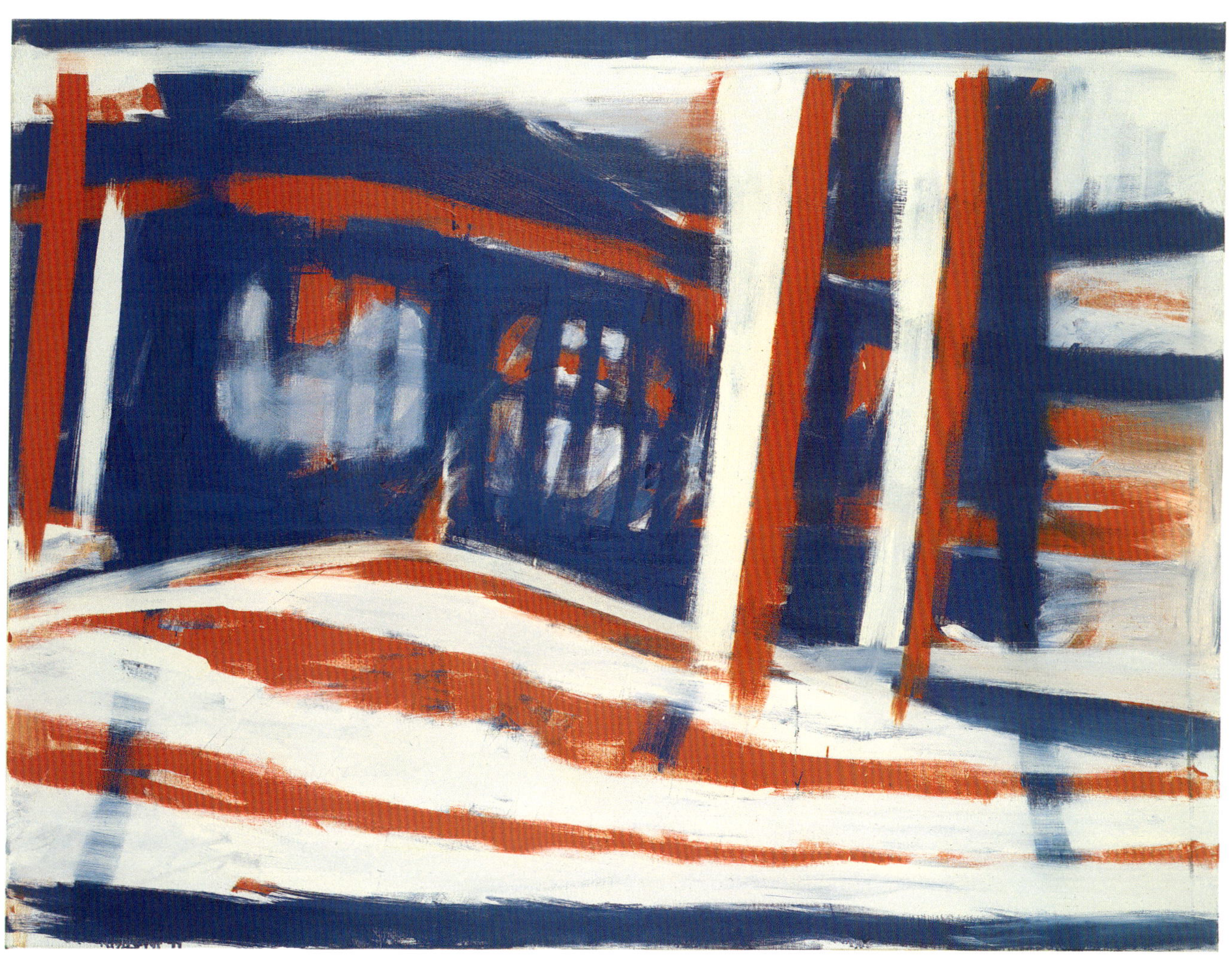

7. *Oh Columbia*, signed, titled and dated 62 on the reverse. Oil on canvas, 62 by 80 in. (157.5 by 203.2 cm.)

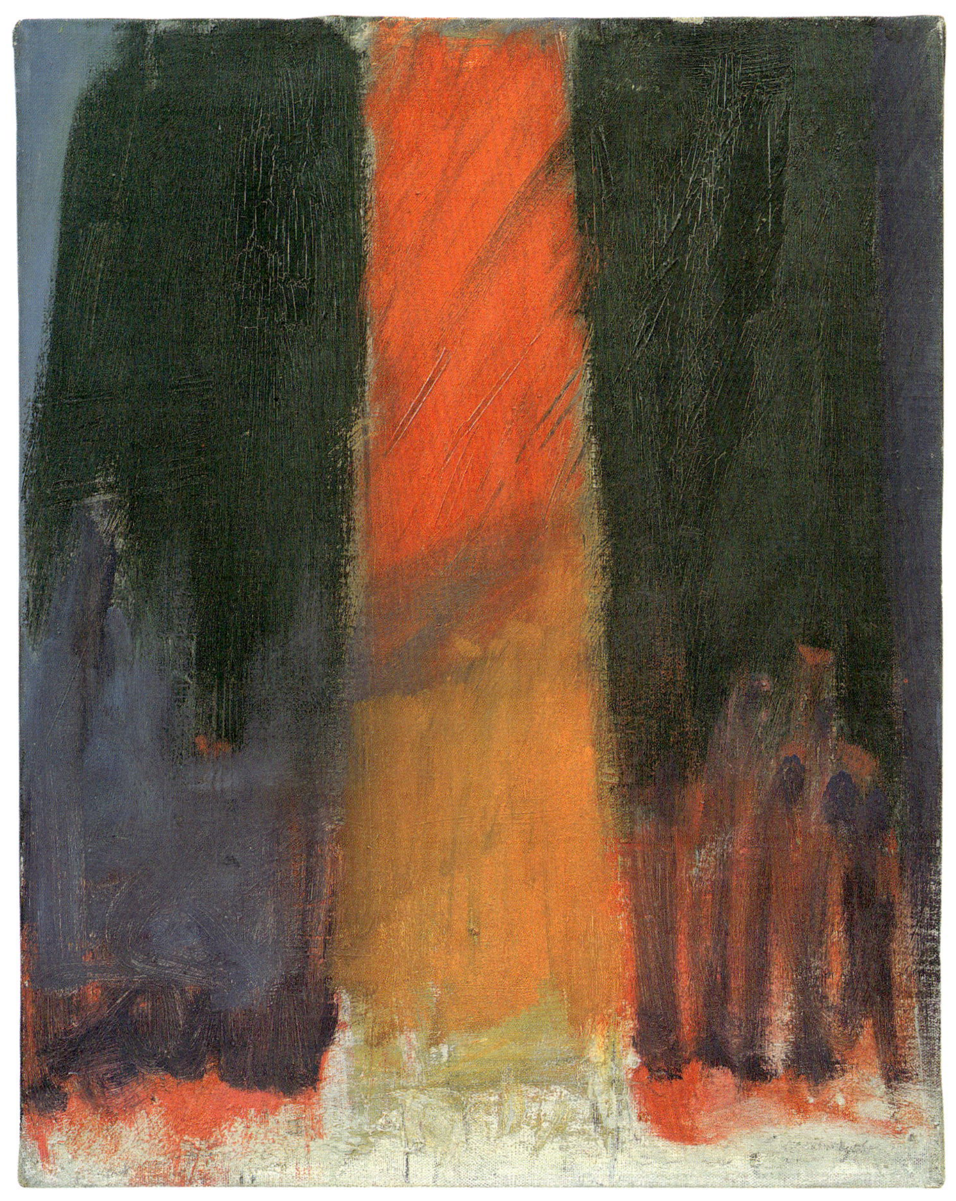

8. *OC #54*, signed, titled and dated *58* on the reverse. Oil on canvas, 18 by 14 in. (45.7 by 35.6 cm.)

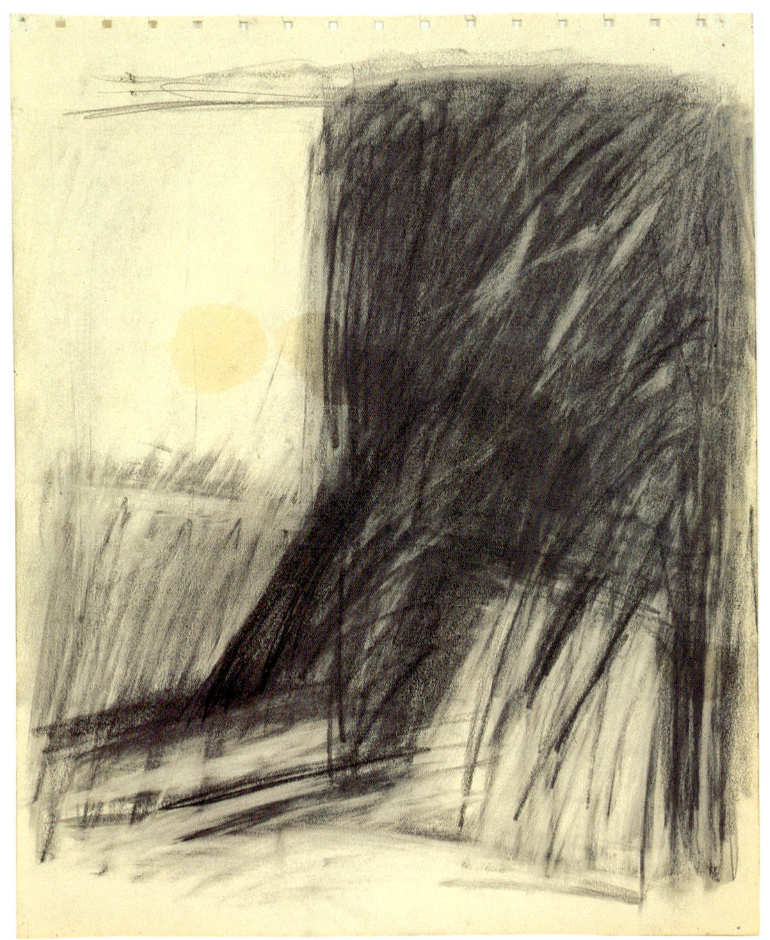

9. *Untitled (Barrier Series)*, circa 1960. Pencil and charcoal on paper, 13⅜ by 10¹³⁄₁₆ in. (34.6 by 27.5 cm.) †

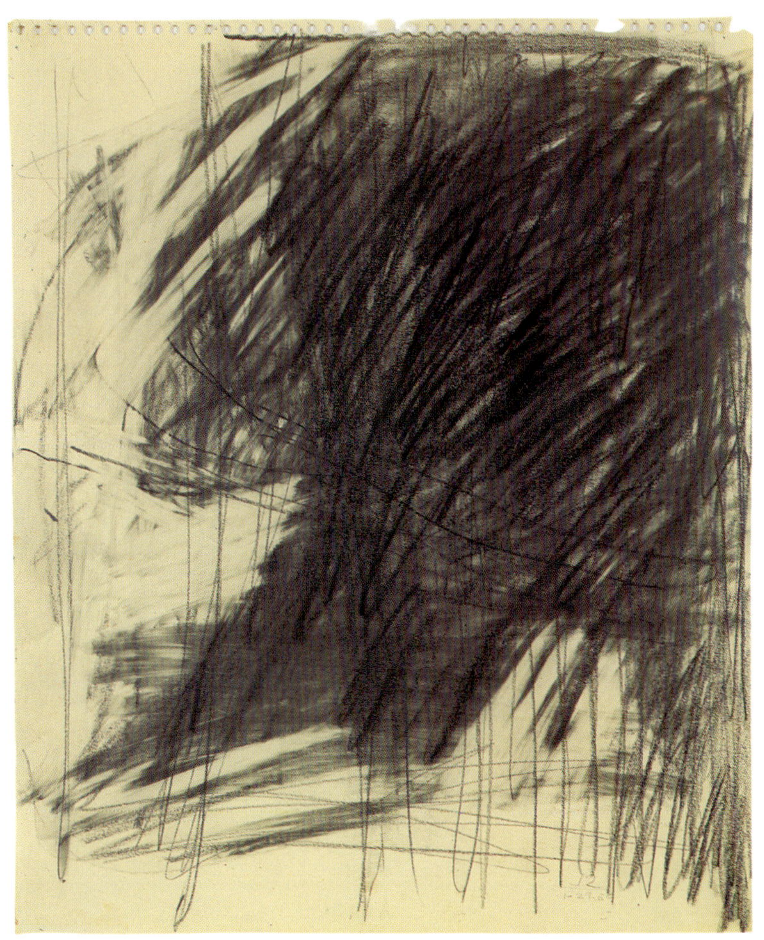

10. *Untitled (Barrier Series)*, signed with initials and dated *1-29-50* [sic ?]. Pencil and charcoal on paper, 13¾ by 11 in. (35 by 27.9 cm.) †

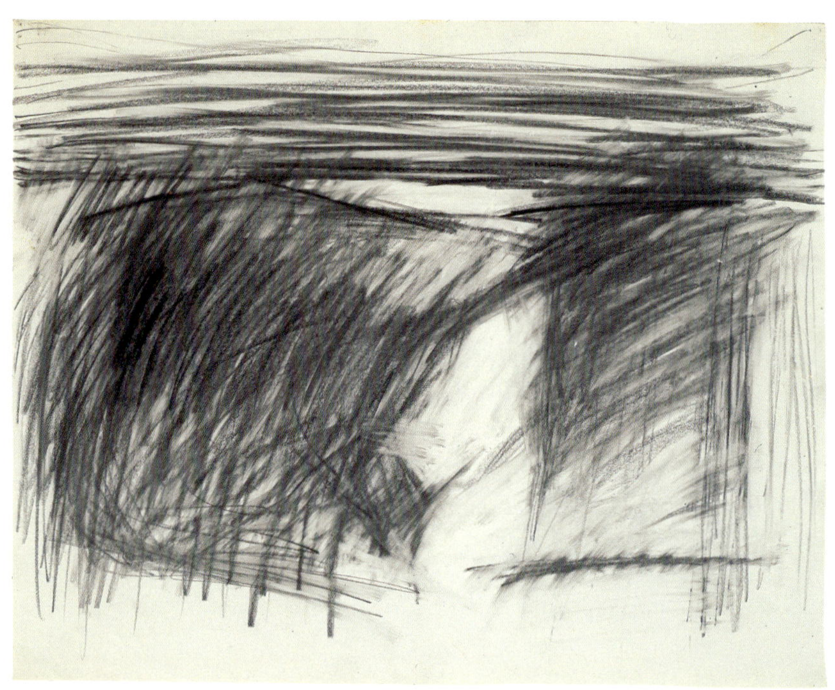

11. *Untitled (Barrier Series),* circa 1960. Pencil and charcoal on paper, 14 by 17 in. (35.6 by 43.2 cm.) †

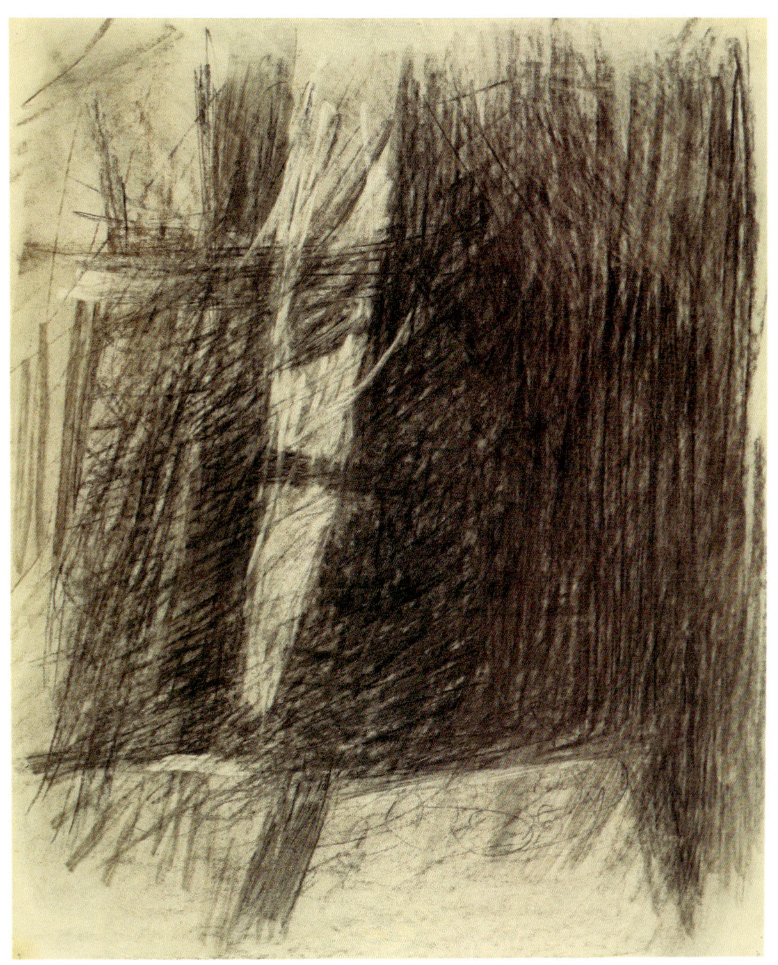

12. *Untitled (Barrier Series)*, circa 1960. Charcoal and conté crayon on paper, 24 by 19⅛ in. (60.9 by 48.3 cm.) †

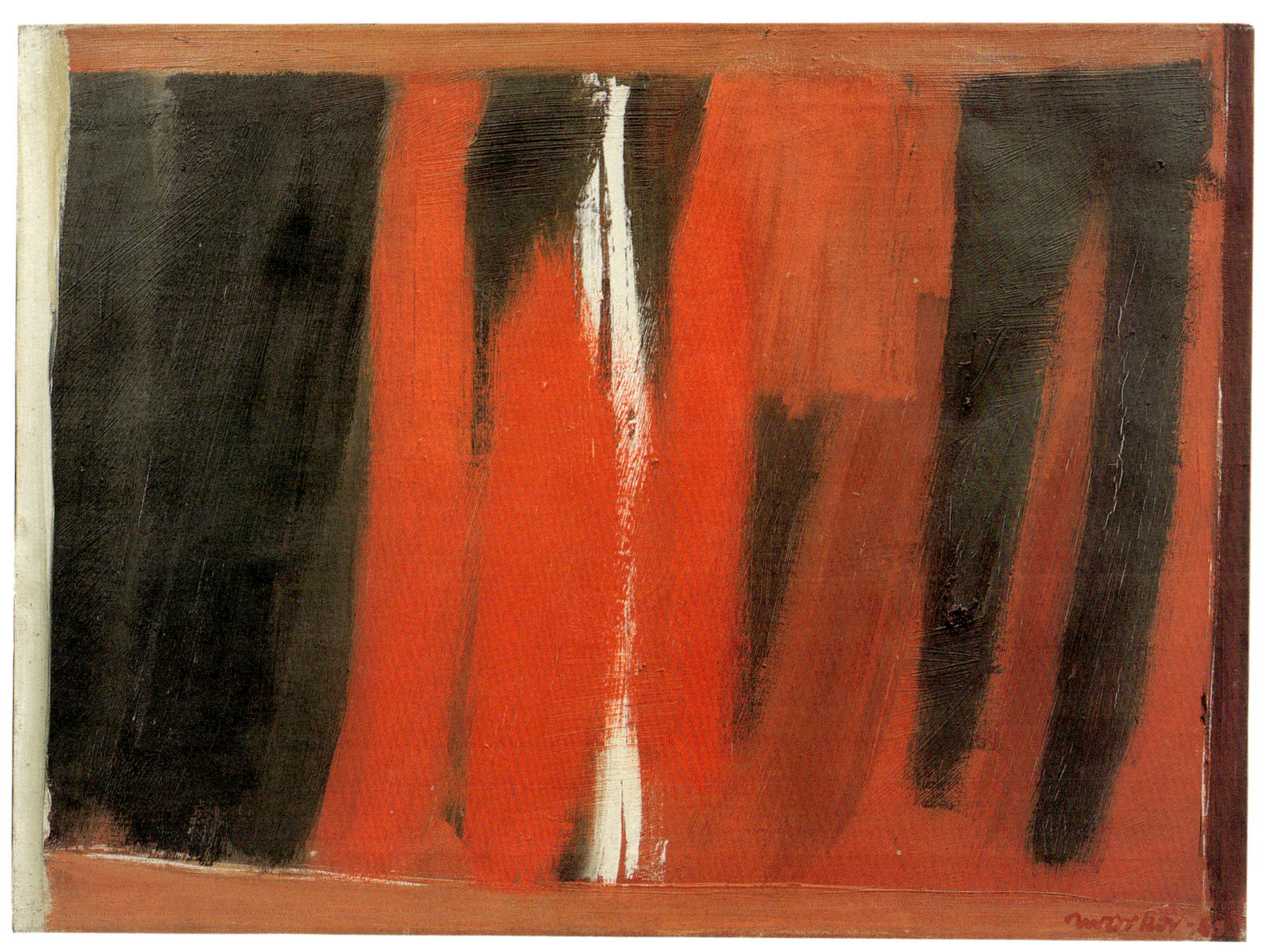

13. *OC #51,* signed, titled and dated *59* on the reverse. Oil on canvas, 18 by 24 in. (45.7 by 61 cm.)

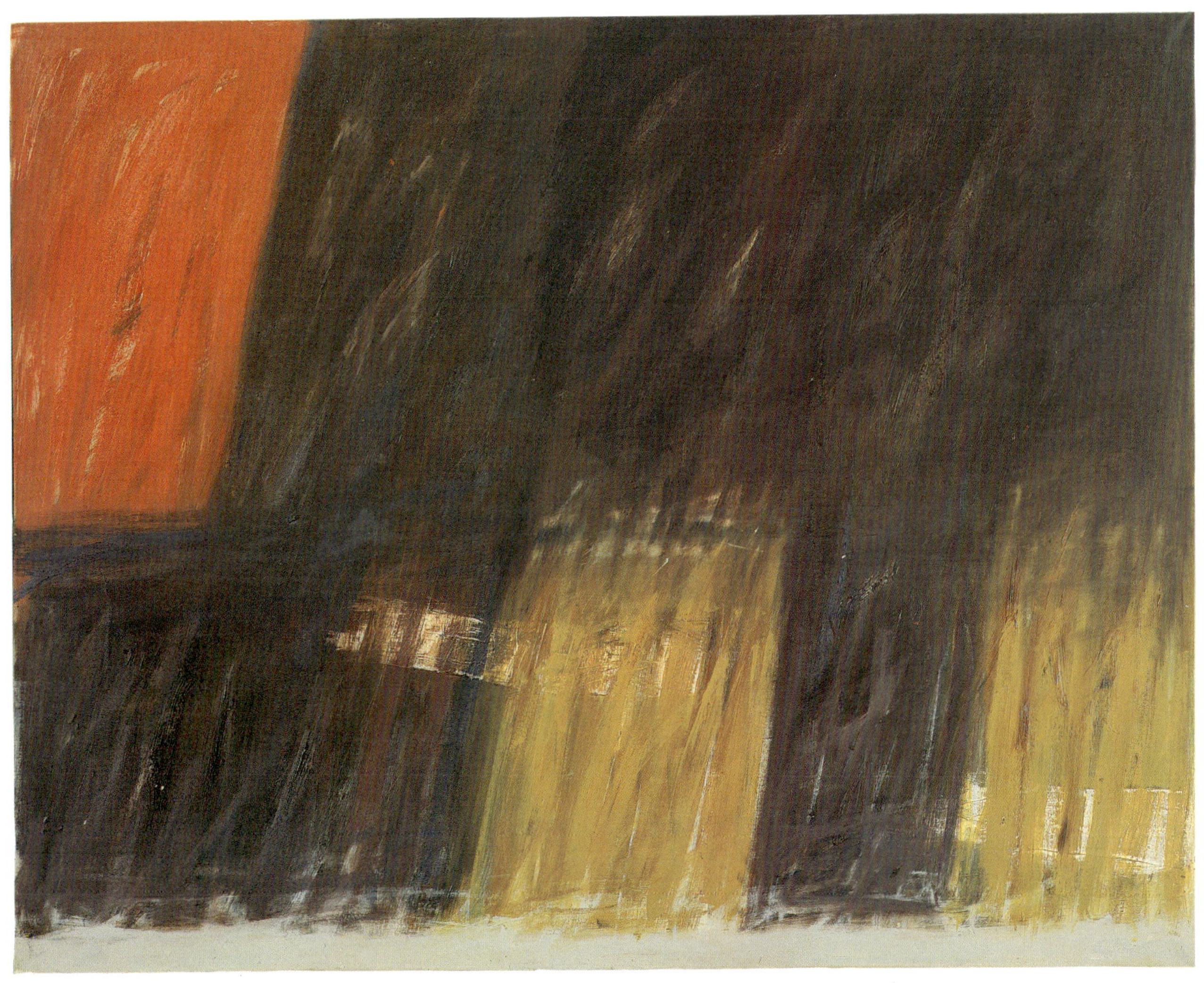

14. *Nightfall*, signed, titled and dated *61* on the reverse. Oil on canvas, 62 by 76 in. (157.5 by 193 cm.)

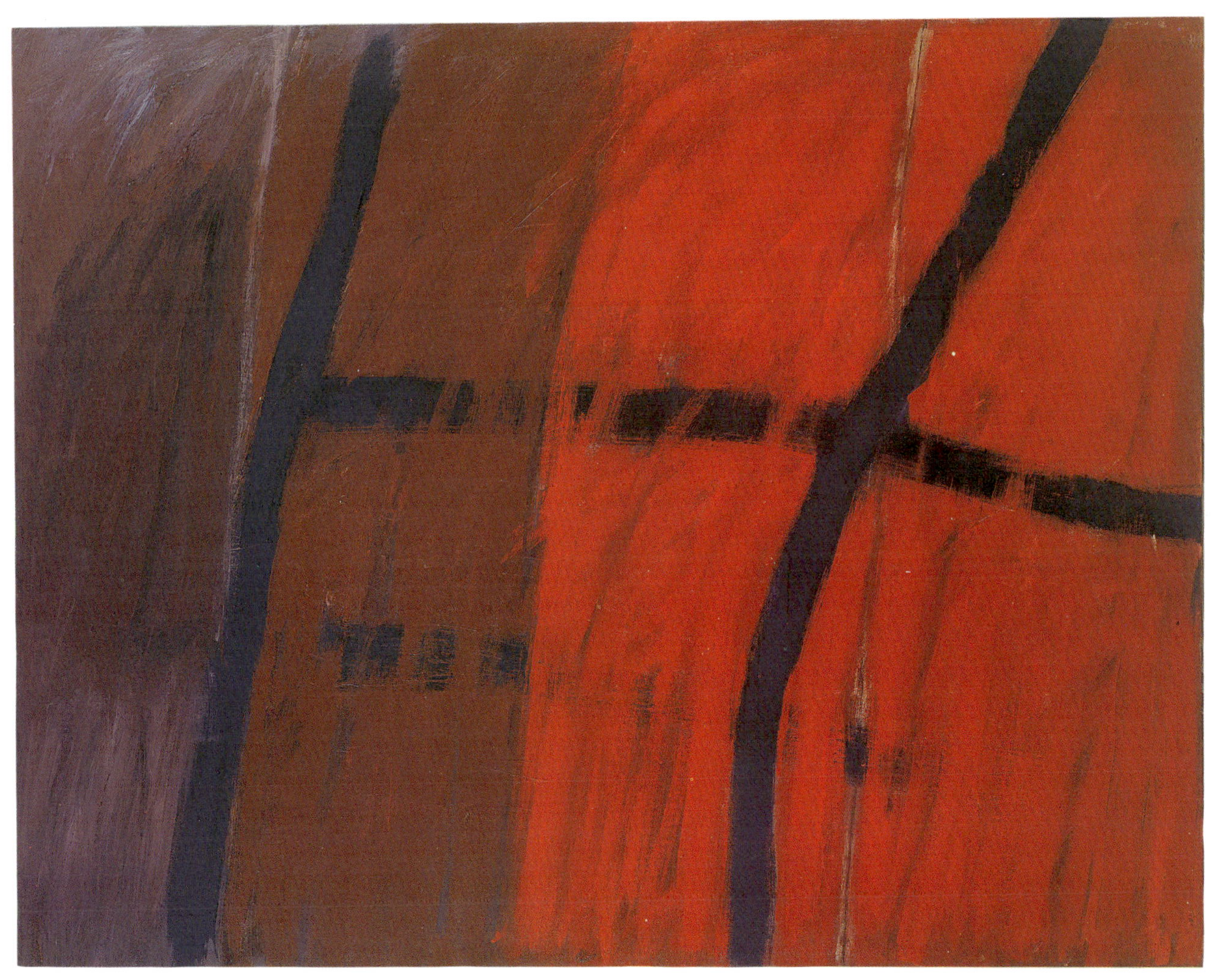

15. *Barrier Series #5*, signed, titled and dated *63* on the reverse. Oil on canvas, 64½ by 80 in. (163.8 by 203.2 cm.)

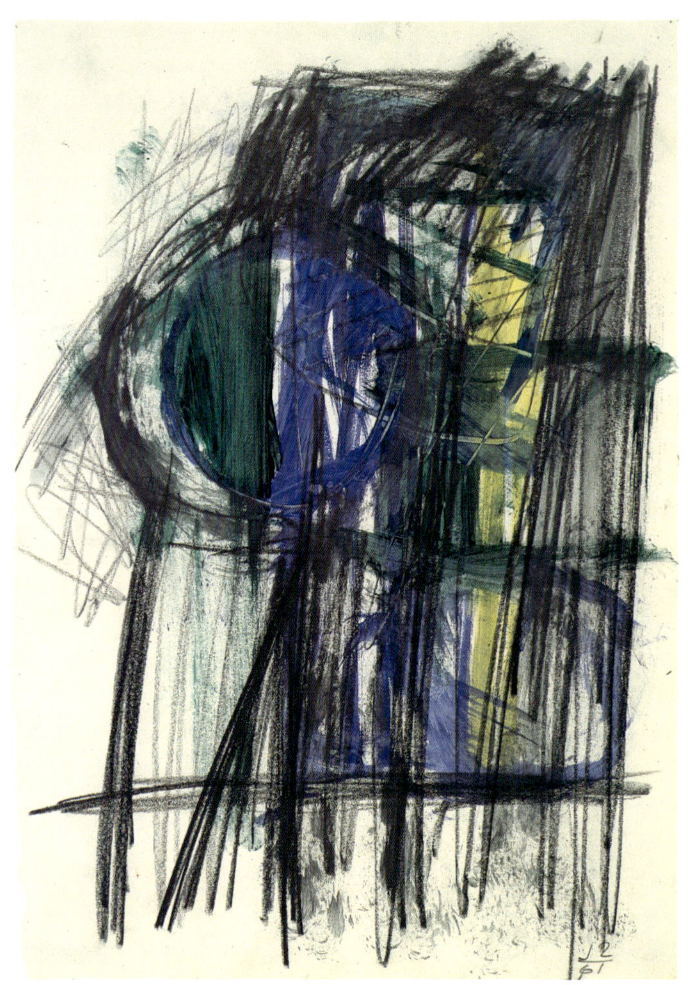
16. *Untitled*, signed with initials and dated *61*. Pencil and liquitex on paper, 22 by 15 in. (55.9 by 38.1 cm.) †

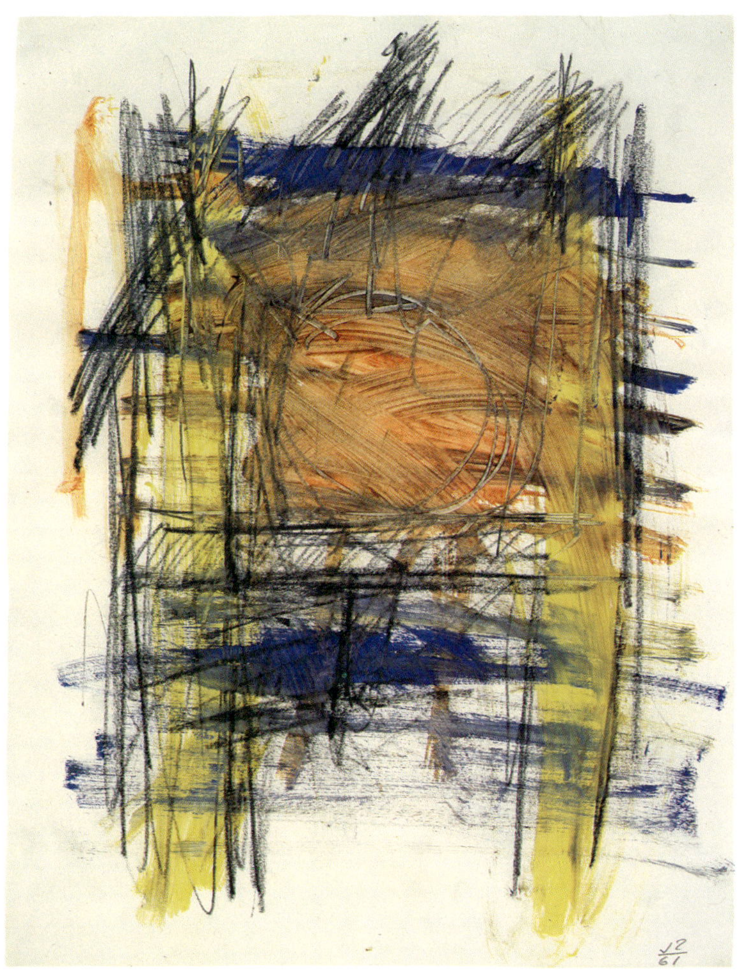

17. *Untitled*, signed with initials and dated *61*. Pencil and liquitex on paper, 24 by 18 in. (61 by 45.7 cm.) †

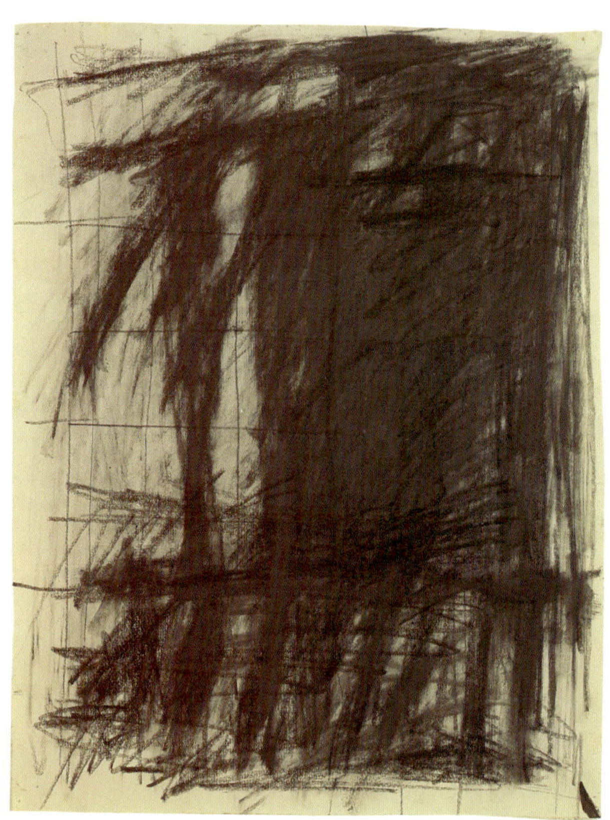

18. *Study for "Site,"* circa 1966. Pencil and charcoal on paper, 15¹⁵⁄₁₆ by 11⅜ in. (38.7 by 29 cm.) †

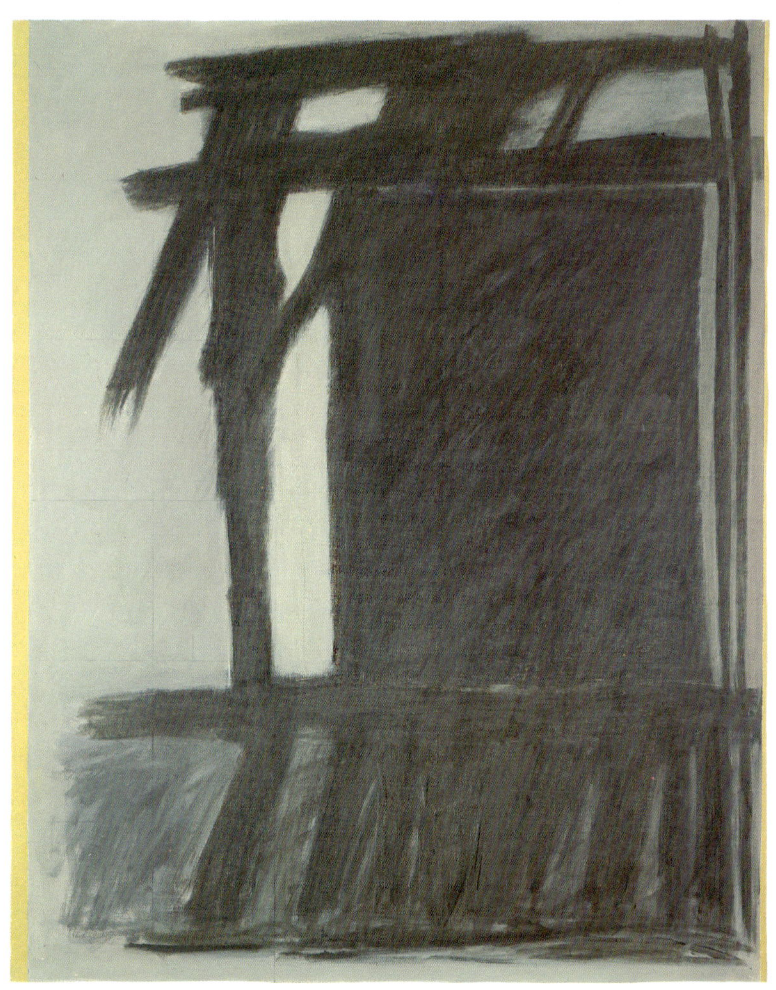

19. *Site*, signed, titled and dated *66* on the reverse. Oil on canvas, 80 by 62 in. (203.2 by 157.5 cm.) †

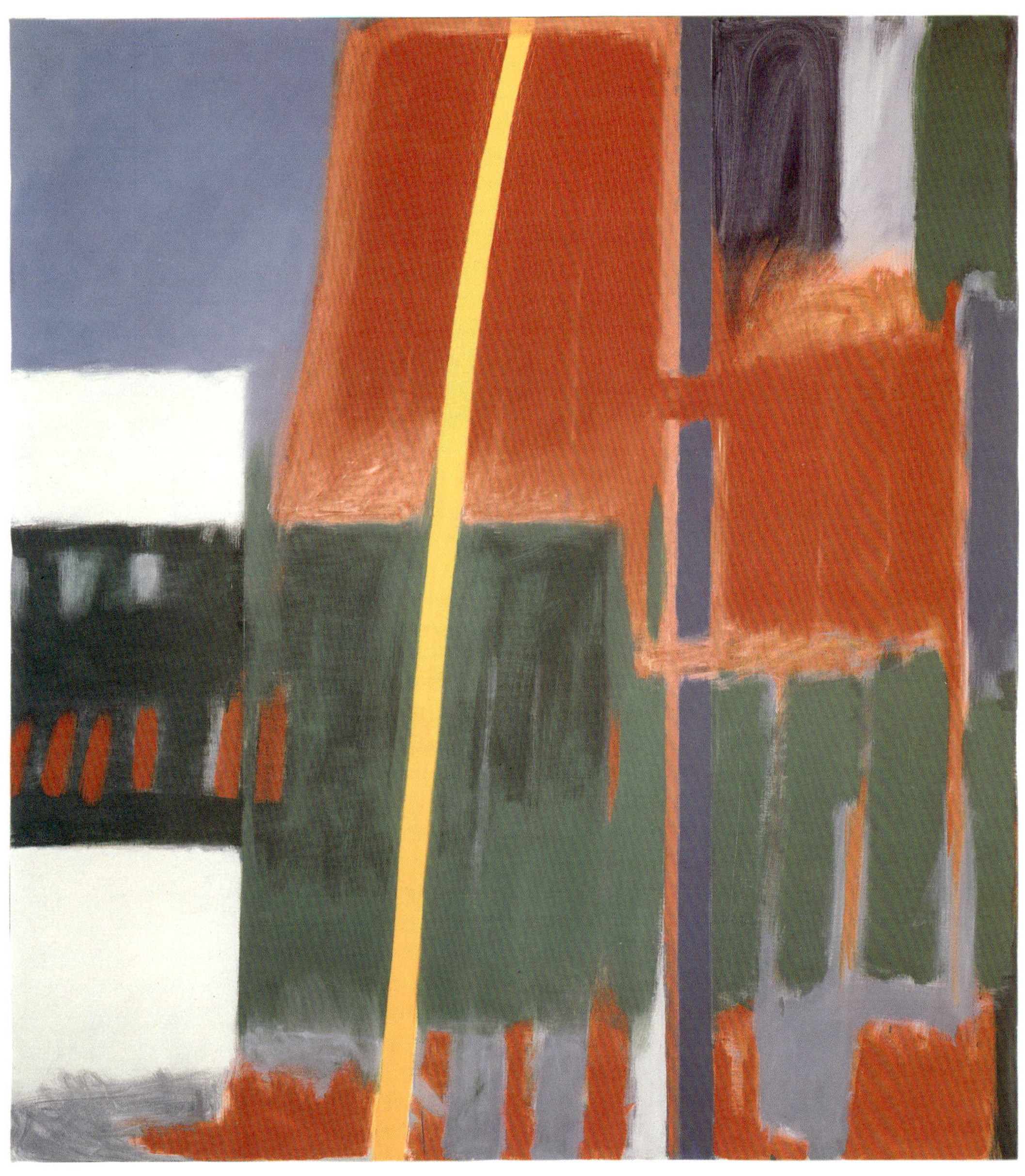

20. *Red & Green with Yellow Stripe*, signed, titled and dated 64 on the reverse. Oil on canvas, 91 by 79 in. (231.1 by 200.6 cm.)

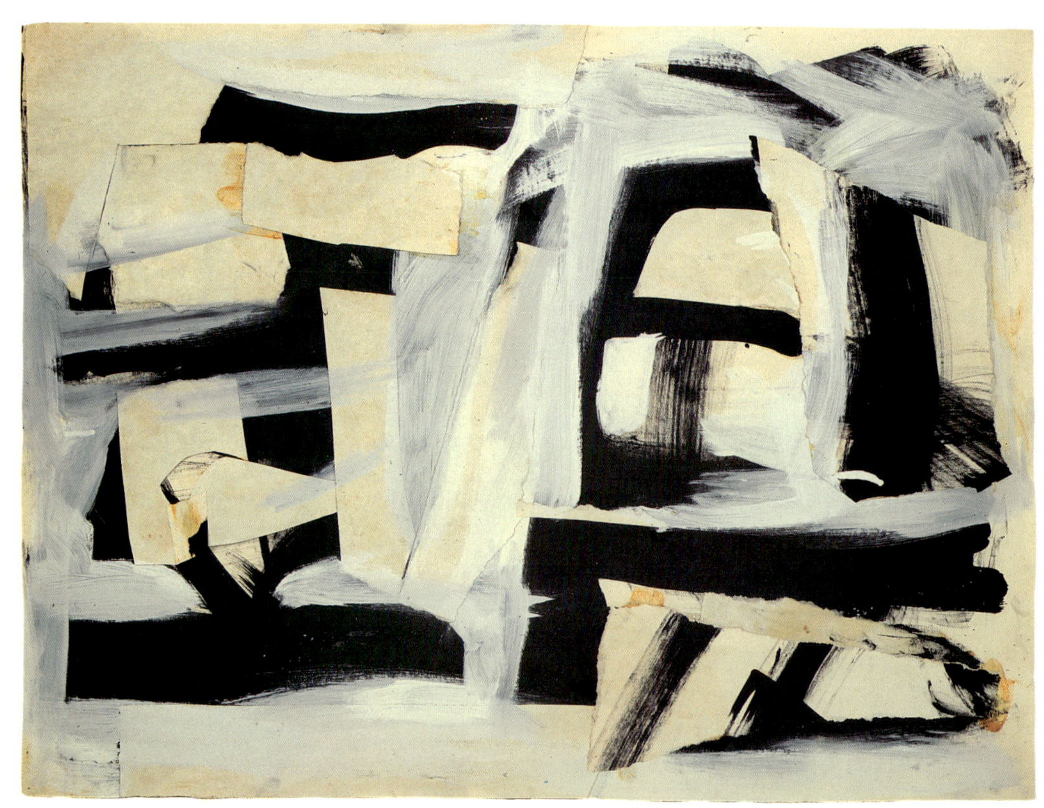

21. *Untitled,* circa 1960–62. Ink and gouache on torn paper collage, 20¹⁄₁₆ by 26¹⁄₁₆ in. (51 by 66.2 cm.) †

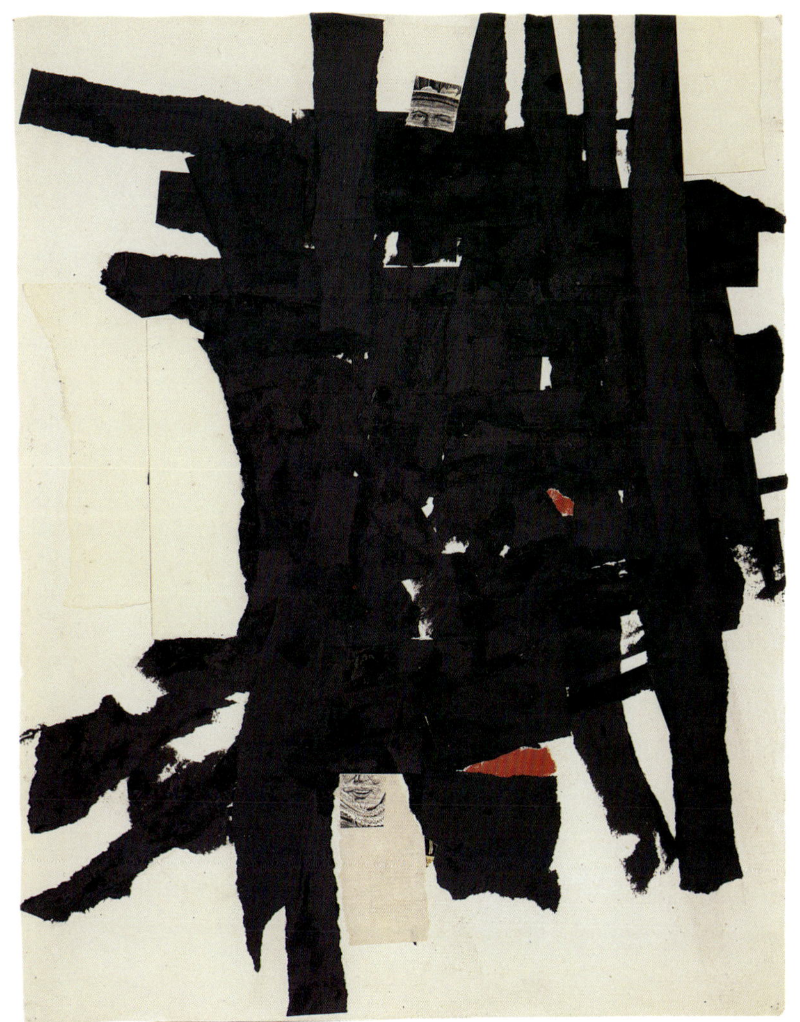

22. *Untitled,* circa 1962–63. Torn paper collage, 20 by 15 in. (50.8 by 38.1 cm.) †

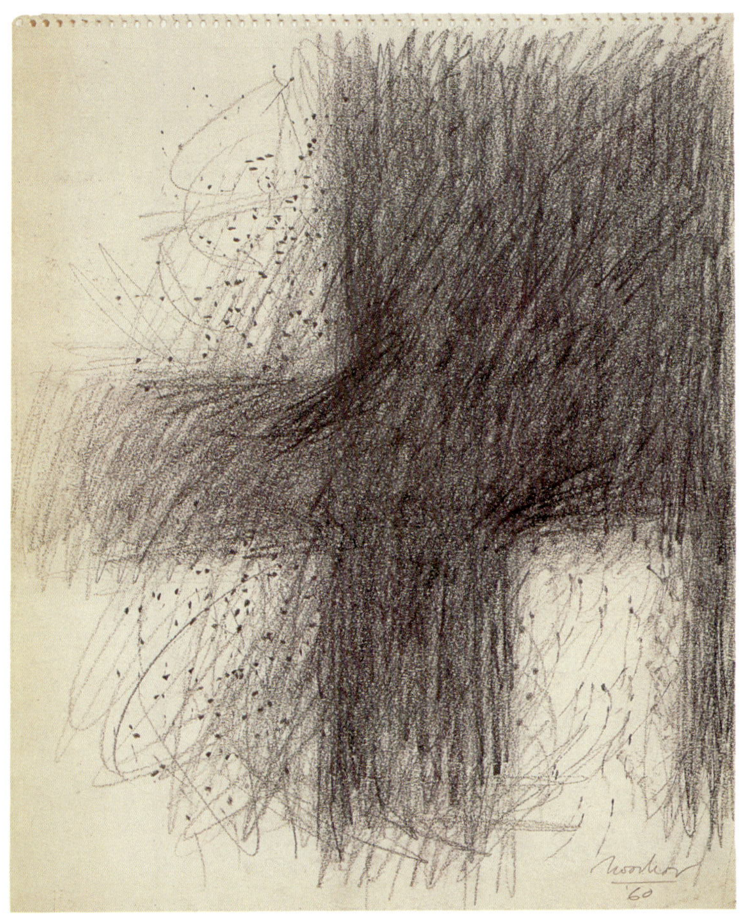

23. *Untitled,* signed and dated 60. Pencil on paper, 13¾ by 11 in. (35 by 27.9 cm.) †

24 *Untitled*, signed with initials and dated 65. Charcoal on paper, 21¹⁵⁄₁₆ by 19 in. (55.7 by 48.4 cm.)

25. *Untitled,* circa 1963–65. Charcoal on paper, 10⅞ by 8⁷⁄₁₆ in. (27.6 by 21.4 cm.)

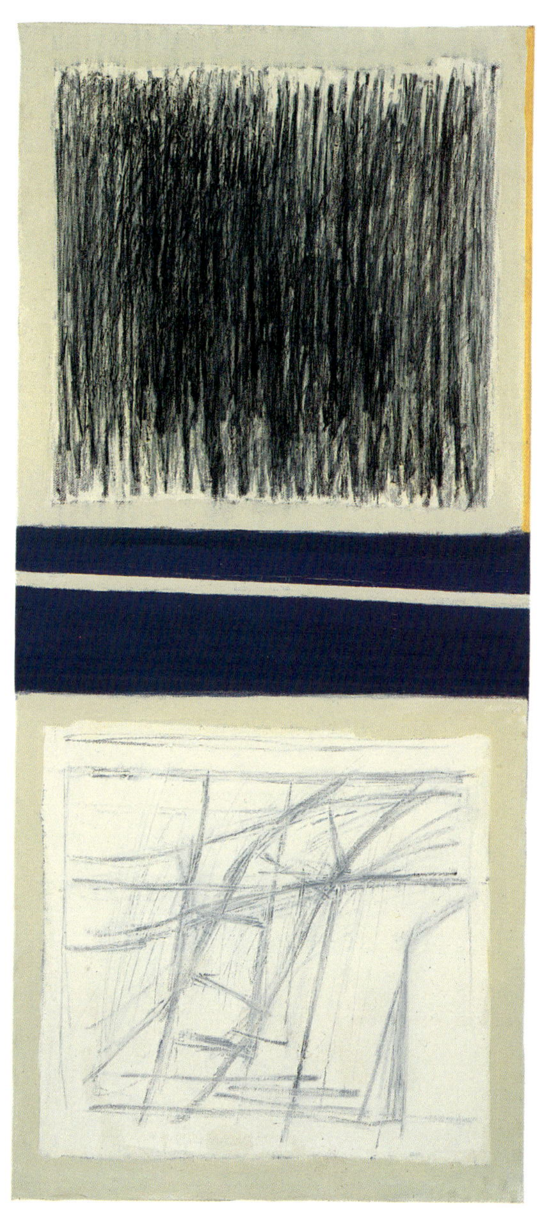

26. *Variables Section I*, signed, titled and dated *63* on the reverse. Oil on canvas, 53½ by 23 in. (135.9 by 58.4 cm.)

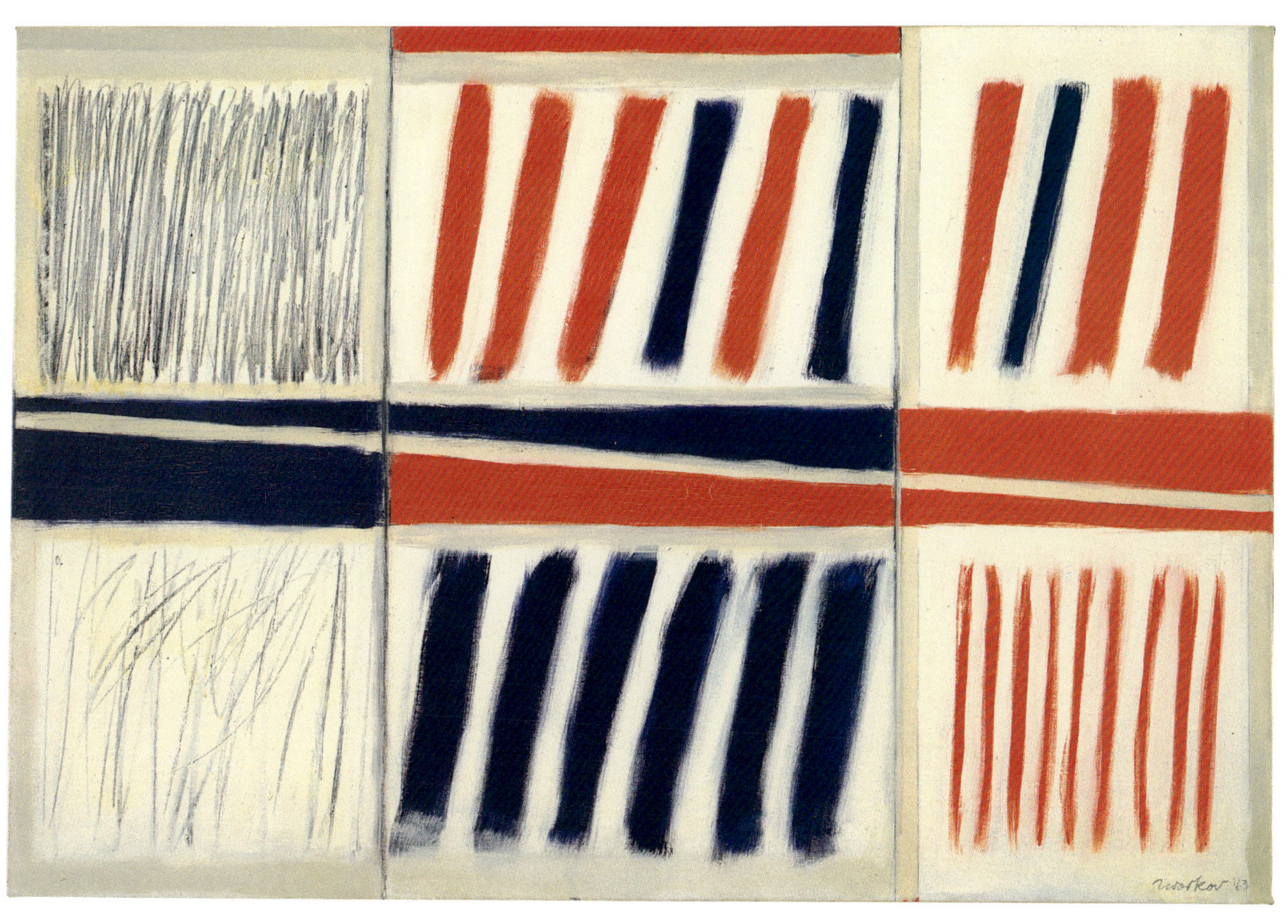

27. *Variables,* signed, titled and dated *63* on the reverse. Oil on canvas, 56 by 80 in. (142.2 by 203.2 cm.)

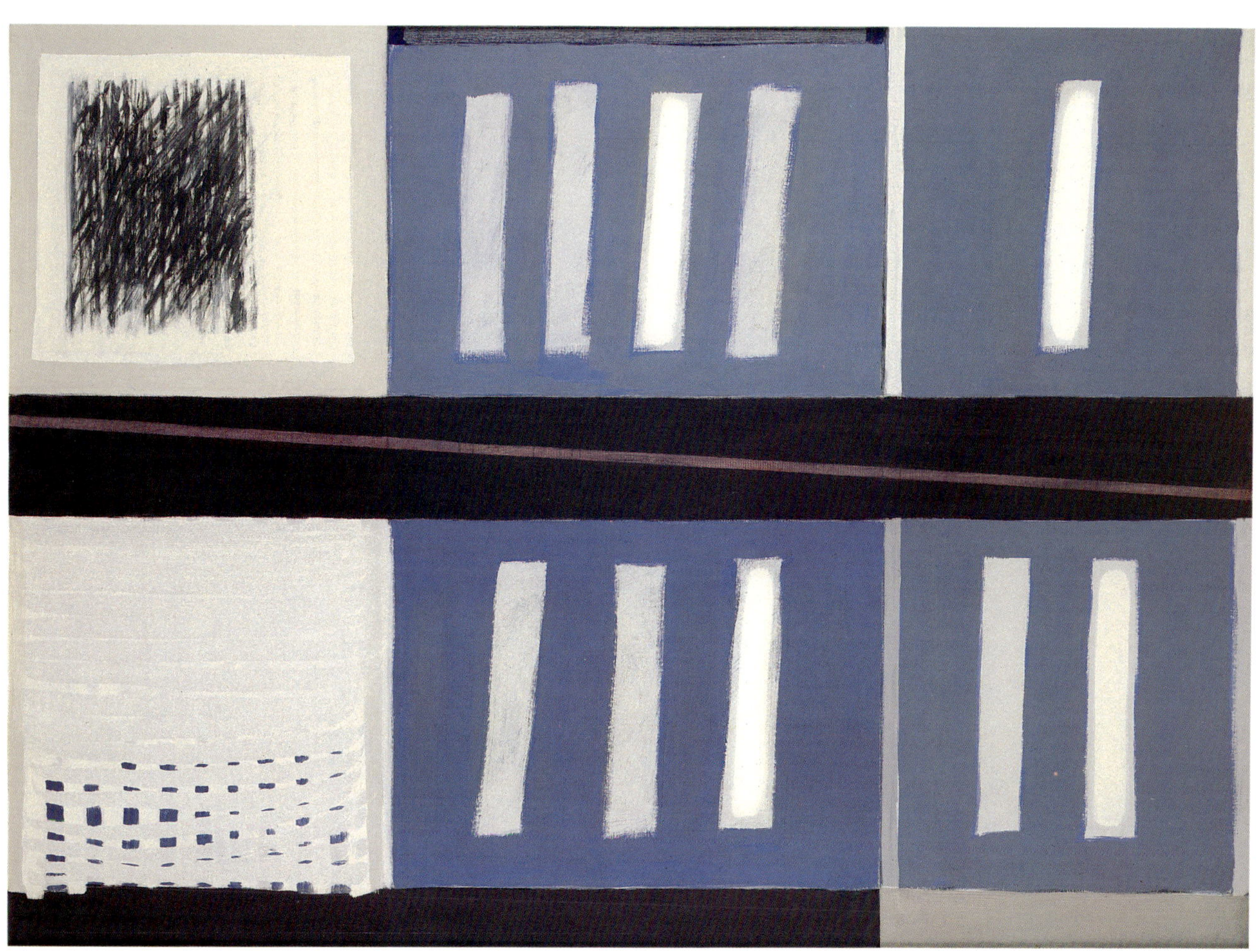

28. *Variables II*, signed, titled and dated 64–65 on the reverse. Oil on canvas, 60 by 80 in. (152.4 by 203.2 cm.)

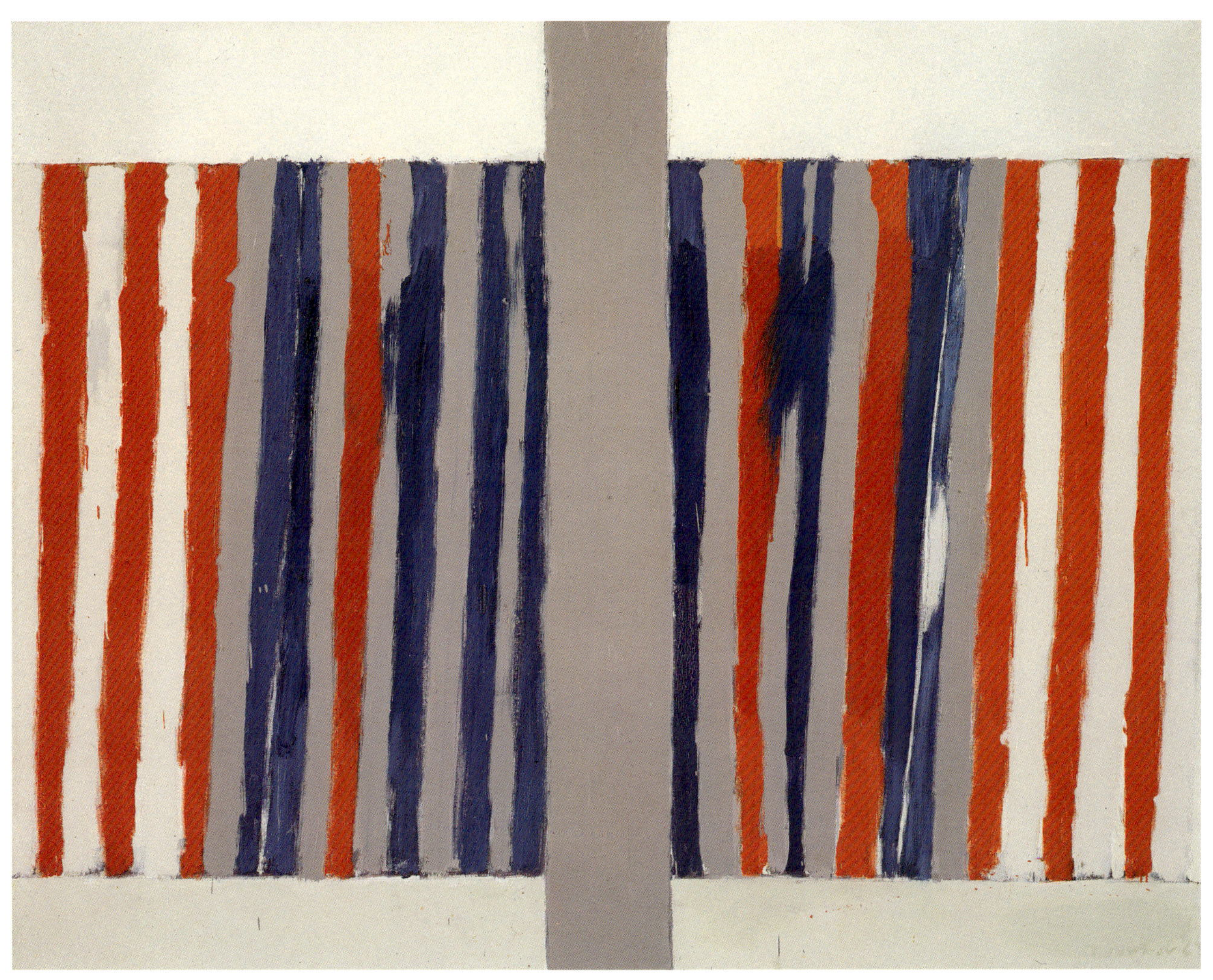

29. *Lane, RWB #4*, signed and dated *63*; signed, titled and dated *63* on the reverse. Oil on canvas, 65 by 80 in. (165.1 by 203.2 cm.) †

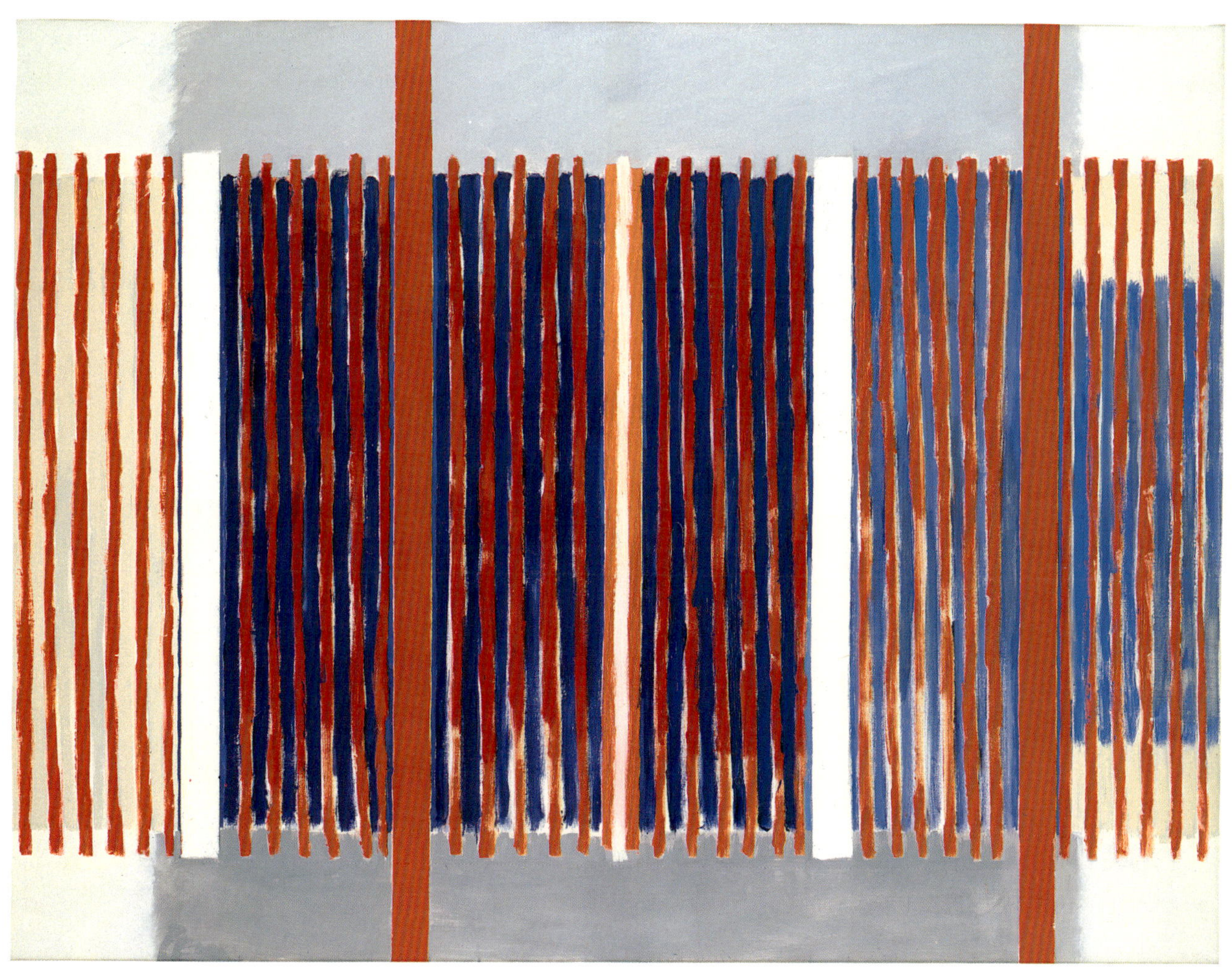

30. *June 11*, signed, titled, inscribed *For Hermine Moskowitz* and dated 64 on the reverse. Oil on canvas, 62 by 80 in. (157.5 by 203.2 cm.) †

31. *Untitled,* circa 1962–63. Torn paper collage, 15 by 20 in. (38.1 by 50.8 cm.) †

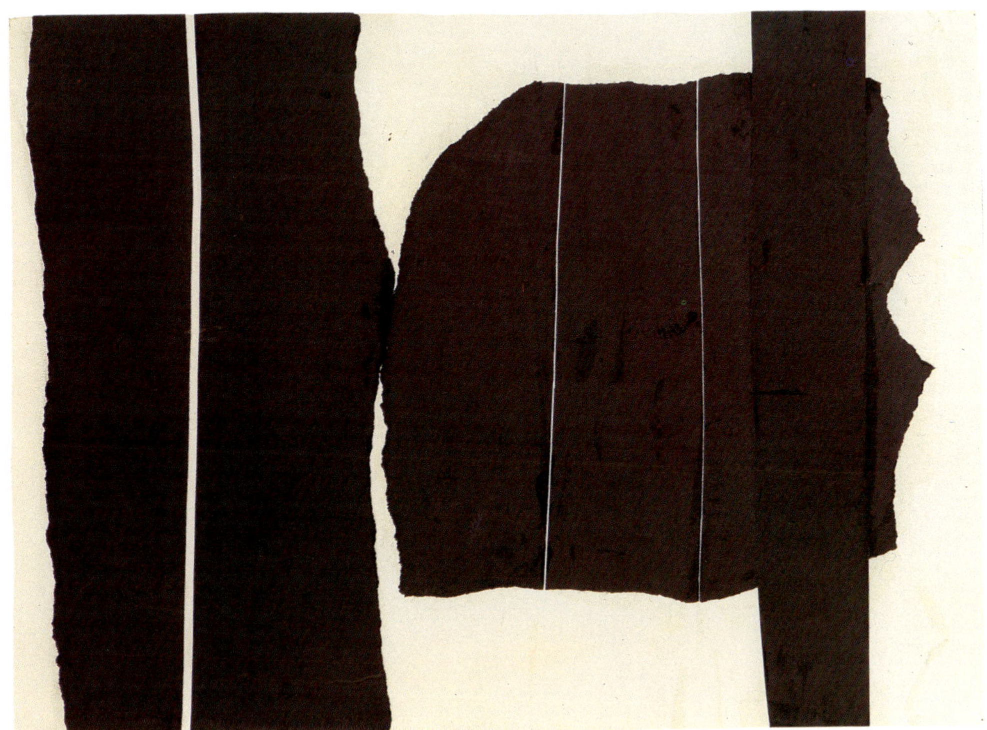

32. *Untitled*, circa 1962–63. Torn paper collage, 15 by 20 in. (38.1 by 50.8 cm.) †

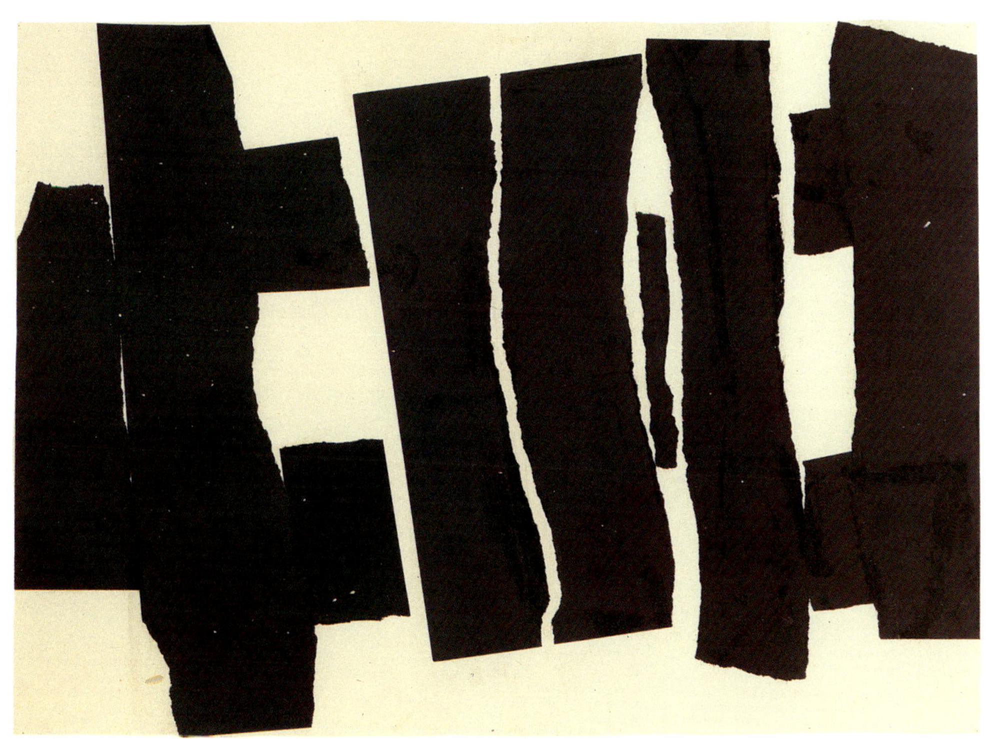

33. *Untitled*, circa 1962–63. Torn paper collage, 15 by 20 in. (38.1 by 50.8 cm.) †

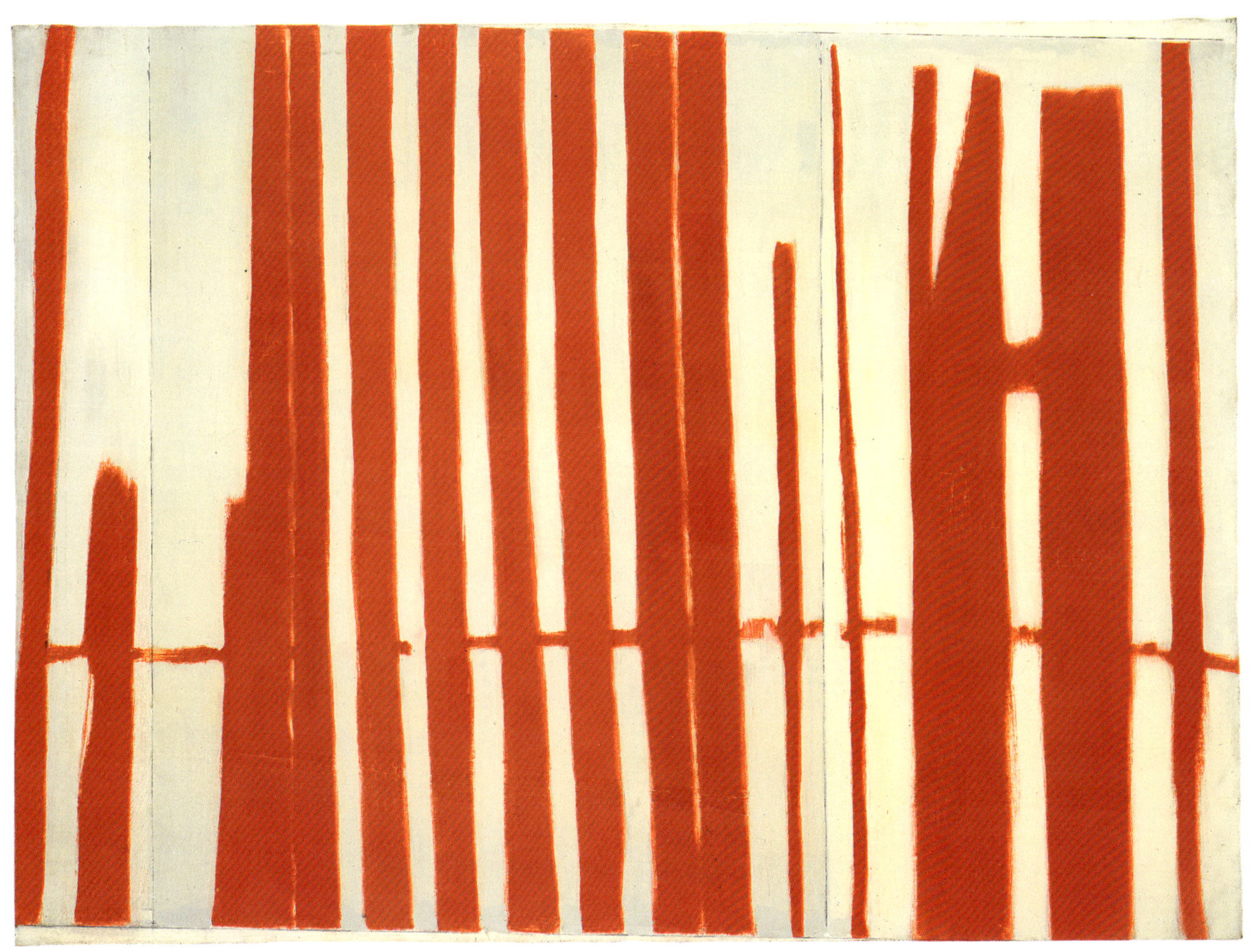

34. *Kin*, signed, titled and dated *63-64* on the reverse. Oil on linen, 60 by 79 in. (152.4 by 200.7 cm)

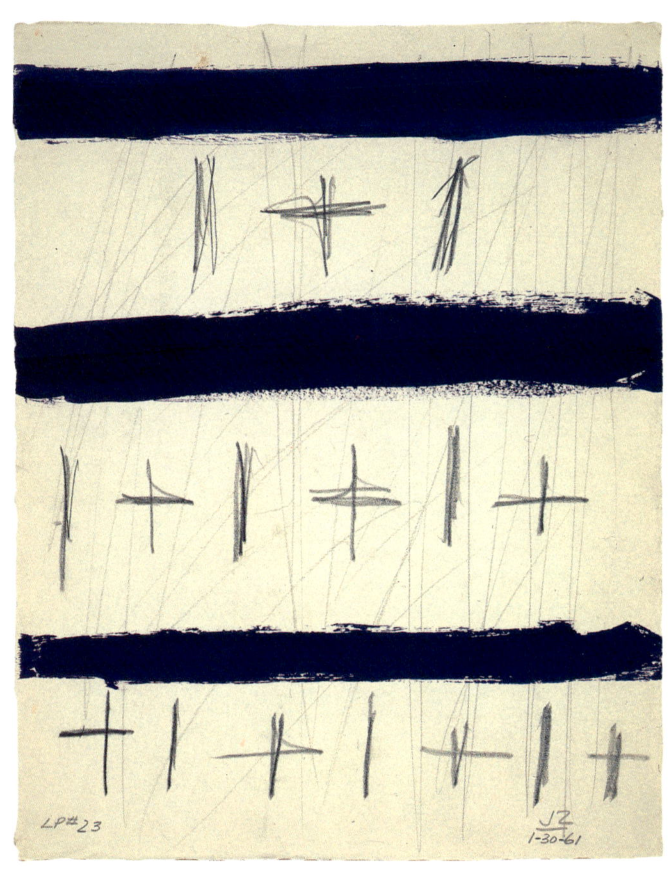

35. *LP #23*, signed with initials, titled and dated *1-30-61*. Pencil and gouache on paper, 13 by 9¹⁵⁄₁₆ in. (33 by 25.2 cm.)

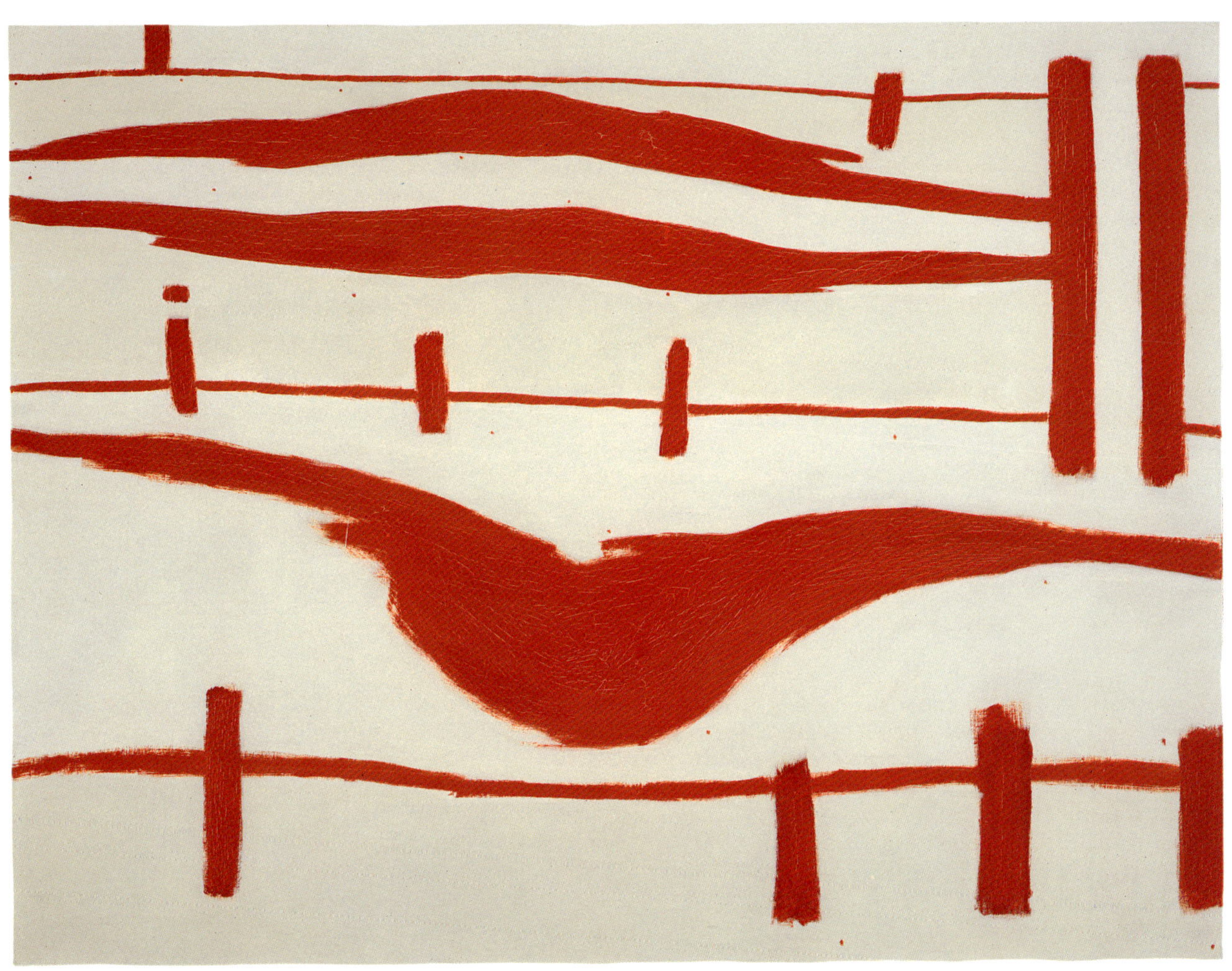

36. *Ebb Tide*, signed, titled and dated 64 on the reverse. Oil on canvas, 63 by 80 in. (160 by 203.2 cm.)

This catalogue accompanies the exhibition
Jack Tworkov: Red, White and Blue
held at Mitchell-Innes & Nash, New York and
Ameringer/Howard/Yohe, New York
from March 6 – April 13, 2002

Mitchell-Innes & Nash
1018 Madison Avneue, New York, NY 10021
T: 212/744 7400 F: 212/744 7401
E: info@miandn.com w: www.miandn.com

Ameringer/Howard/Yohe
20 West 57th Street, New York, NY 10019
T: 212/445 0051 F: 212/445 0102
E: nycgallery@ameringer-howard.com w: www.artnet.com

Cover: Jack Tworkov, *Oh Columbia* (detail, cat. no. 7)

Publication © Mitchell-Innes & Nash and
Ameringer/Howard/Yohe
Images of Jack Tworkov © The Estate of Jack Tworkov,
   New York
Essay © Harry Cooper

ISBN: 0-9713844-4-4

Photography: Tom Powel Imaging
Design: Lawrence Sunden, Inc.
Printing: The Studley Press
Printed and bound in the United States

Available through D.A.P./Distributed Art Publishers
155 Sixth Avenue, 2nd Floor, New York, NY 10013
T: 212/627 1999 F: 212/627 9484

Mitchell-Innes & Nash and Ameringer/Howard/Yohe would like
to thank Hermine Ford and Helen Tworkov for their enthusiasm
during this project. We are especially grateful to them for making
available the artist's journals, as they have proven to be enor-
mously revealing and have helped provide fresh insights into
Tworkov's theoretical and political thinking. Thanks as well to
Jeri Coppola, the estate curator, for her invaluable research. To
Harry Cooper, with whom it has been a pleasure to work, and
whose insightful and ambitious essay has brought to light new
aspects of Tworkov's painting, we extend our deepest apprecia-
tion. And as always, we thank John Silberman, lawyer for the
Tworkov estate, for his support of this exhibition.